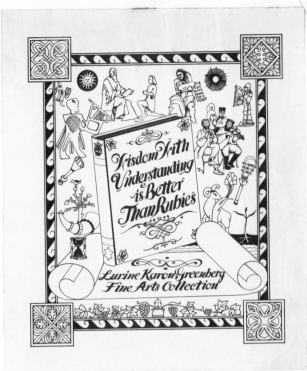

Wisdom With
Understanding
is Better
Than Rubies

Lurine Karon Greenberg
Fine Arts Collection

Creating a
CHINESE
GARDEN

Creating a
CHINESE
GARDEN

Foreword by Sir Harold Acton

David H. Engel

Croom Helm, London
Timber Press, Portland, Oregon

© 1986 David H. Engel
Croom Helm Ltd, Provident House, Burrell Row,
Beckenham, Kent BR3 1AT

British Library Cataloguing in Publication Data

Engel, David
    Creating a Chinese Garden.
    1. Gardens, Chinese
    712'06   SB457.55
    ISBN 0-7099-0977-2

First published in the USA in 1986 by
Timber Press
9999 SW Wilshire
Portland, Oregon 97225

ISBN 0-88192-025-8

Typeset in Goudy Old Style by Leaper & Gard Ltd, Bristol
Printed and bound in Great Britain by The Bath Press

Contents

Colour Plates

Figures

To Bruno K. Piantoni who inspired this book

Set high and deep among the hills
Stands Magic City
Leaning upon the void; its towers
Invade the realm of gods.
Beyond, a bright moon voyages
Through a cloudless autumn sky;
But the world below is darkened by
Fine rain like springtime mist.
A dragon from the sky swoops down.

Wang Yangming
'Magic City Monastery'

Acknowledgements

I began work on this book in 1978. During the intervening years I was encouraged by my business partner, Dennis H. Piermont, to take time away from our landscape architectural practice, ENGEL/GGP, to do the research, travel and writing that was necessary to complete the work. For his patience and understanding I express my gratitude. My thanks also to Laura Ho for her translations.

Photographic Credits

The photographs of gardens were taken by the author in China in 1982 and 1983. The one exception is Figure 3.21, which was taken by Mary Lou Estabrook of the *Lakeville Journal*, Lakeville, Connecticut. Credits for the reproductions of the Chinese garden paintings follow: Figures 1.14 and 3.42: *The Garden for Self Enjoyment*: The Cleveland Museum of Art, Purchase, John L. Severance Fund. Figure 1.11: *Purification At The Orchid Pavilion*: The Cleveland Museum of Art, Gift of the Junior Council of the Cleveland Museum of Art, and of Mrs Wai-kam Ho in the name of the Junior Council. Figure 3.49: *The Literary Gathering At A Yangzhou Garden*: The Cleveland Museum of Art, Purchase, The Severance and Greta Millikin Purchase Fund. Figure 1.1: *The Gazing Garden*: The Metropolitan Museum of Art, gift of Constance Tang Fong, in honour of Mrs P.Y. Tang, 1982.

David Harris Engel

Foreword

Sir Harold Acton

The traditional Chinese garden differs in many respects from those to which Westerners are accustomed, yet gardens exist in the West which have been visibly inspired by Chinese landscape art. The American painter, Walter Beck, never visited China but he was influenced by a Tang dynasty scroll, attributed to the great painter-poet, Wang Wei, to emulate his portrayal of a Chinese garden. At Millbrook, New York, the cups of his 'Cup Garden' called Innisfree are in the form of rockeries, with fern-fringed waterfalls, stepping-stones, lotus pools and zigzag bridges. But this is a garden covering a thousand acres of wooded hills around an azure lake, whereas the average Chinese garden is comparatively small — the famous Wang Shi Yuan at Suzhou covers one and a third acres — and Japanese gardens are even smaller in proportion and extent. Walter Beck was fascinated by the strange rocks characteristic of Chinese gardens, and he was able to find substitutes in the neighbouring hillsides.

No doubt 'Innisfree' is exceptional, but David Engel's book, *Creating a Chinese Garden*, should promote the creation of Chinese gardens, both in the country and in the heart of cities for rest and relaxation. He has provided a valuable guide to Chinese garden planning and practice, design and construction techniques and, what we may seek in vain elsewhere, an annotated plant list arranged in categories with English and Chinese names. As many of these plants are cultivated in Europe and America, Mr Engel's list will prove useful to enterprising gardeners who wish to seek out interesting and unusual varieties. The splendid cryptomeria and the prehistoric ginkgo are fairly uncommon in Europe, but I have seen fine specimens of the latter flourishing in the grounds of Birr Castle, Offaly, in Ireland, whose climate, thanks to the Gulf Stream, is favourable to exotics. Unfortunately our elms are an endangered species, as are the columnar cypresses of Tuscany now threatened by industrial pollution.

Our Western gardens, especially in England, are mainly horticultural, and, as the author points out, 'the Chinese garden is not essentially of horticultural interest with a profusion of plants growing in wild abandon'. This also applies to the formal gardens of Italy where the layout is symmetrical, though here, too, flowers 'are grown in pots and tubs that are shifted with their blooming seasons'.

To evoke the beauties of natural scenery on an intimate scale is the aim of the Chinese gardener. These beauties are familiar to connoisseurs of Chinese painting. Their term for landscape is *Shan-shui*, 'mountain-and-stream', symbolising all aspects of nature. Consequently, the gardener manipulates rocks and flowing water so that images of great mountains and rivers are conjured up within a limited area.

Trees and plants are subsidiary: they are selected for their shapes and colours, as well as their symbolism, to harmonise with the locality. Rocks and their arrangement are of salient importance: these are the abstract equivalents of statues in Europe. The rarest, from Tai-hu, are mounted on carved pedestals of marble. As Mr Engel observes, they are valued for 'their bizarrerie of shape and for their capacity to suggest remote and mythical places —' or Buddhist Immortals and fabulous animals.

Meandering paths, cobbled paving, mossy steps, rippling streams under zigzag bridges, 'miniature mountains' and open pavilions for contemplation — all are based on the harmonious balance of *yin*, the yielding watery female element interpreted as negative, and *yang*, the tough masculine rock, interpreted as positive (to the annoyance of modern feminists).

At Wang Shi Yuan a lake is 'balanced' or framed by the intricate rockery known as 'miniature mountains'. This exquisite garden is situated in the middle of a bustling city — a retreat from the madding crowd which we would be wise to emulate. Why should we not take a hint from the Chinese and build similar oases in our modern cities?

David Engel points the way and provides us with the technical details in his thought-provoking book. His chapter on the affinities and contrasts between Chinese and Japanese gardens, superficially akin, is of particular interest to those of us who find them hard to distinguish. To my eye, Japanese gardens seem pastiches of their Chinese prototypes. A certain knowledge of Zen Buddhism is required fully to savour their subtleties. Mr Engel concludes that 'Japanese gardens are much more impersonal: the Japanese prize rougher surfaces and textures, less colour, bare, aged wood.' Simplicity, austerity even a veneer of rusticity, in the use of thatched roofs for instance, are the keynotes. The author makes a felicitous comparison between 'the plain and neutral patterns and earth-tones of *raku* pottery bowls and the refinement of Sung celadon bowls.' I should add a studied casualness and reticence — apart from the diminished scale and cult of dwarf plants, for the Japanese are highly skilled in flower arrangement in and out of doors. But here we enter the realm of metaphysics. A plot of carefully raked grey sand with a few dark stones may inspire meditations on infinity. Chinese gardens are indeed roccoco in comparison!

All Chinese painting derives from Chinese calligraphy, for the written character was the earliest form of a picture. As a picture gains intensity when it is accompanied by a poem, the glory of a garden is enhanced by tablets inscribed with an appropriate verse or aphorism. Even if the meaning eludes us we cannot fail to admire the abstract beauty of the brush-work. The style of the calligraphy should blend with the rocks and water and vegetation. Usually it provides a commentary on the scene and commemorates some historical association, illuminating the general composition. Our Italic or

Gothic script does not lend itself to such purposes for it bears little relation to painting. The most significant lines of our poetry, such as 'a thing of beauty is a joy forever', would look prosaic in an English garden. No matter how neat the inscription, no Western poet could embellish a landscape with a poem. Our inscriptions on boards are usually warnings to keep off the grass or arrows pointing to an exit. Our sun-dials are probably the nearest equivalent to the Chinese tablets, for they are sometimes engraved with mottoes, cheerfully reminding us of the flight of time, the brevity of human life.

Confucius said: 'The wise take pleasure in rivers and lakes, the virtuous in mountains.' I do not know how Confucius stands in the People's Republic of today, but it is certain that the wise and the virtuous meet happily in the surviving gardens of ancient China, where rivers, lakes and mountains may be enjoyed without risk or fatigue. Mr Engel has emphasised their escapist element, but do not all gardens provide an escape from world-weariness and care?

The love of gardens should form a spiritual bond between East and West. We have so much to learn from each other, and it is a comfort to know that the gardens of the Summer Palace near Peking, of Yu Yuan in Shanghai, besides those of Suzhou and Wuxi near Lake Tai, have been scrupulously restored and renovated since the depredations of the so-called Cultural Revolution. Fortunately, the appreciation of wild mountain scenery is a national characteristic, even if the former respect for scholars and *literati* has been mitigated by Marxist theory.

For a former resident of Peking like myself *Creating a Chinese Garden* kindles memories of unique aesthetic experiences which I hope will be shared by future visitors to China. Mr Engel seems to promise the realisation of that hope. While recommending his book I regard him as a pioneering aesthetic missionary.

Sir Harold Acton
Florence, Italy

Chapter I
Introduction:
The Chinese Garden
Characterised

The Chinese Garden Characterised

To enter a Chinese garden is to gain admittance into an idealised world of imagination and fantasy that reveals itself, step by step, to the wanderer among its man-made hills and valleys, and walled-in courtyards. Treading the undulating pathways and pavements of pebble mosaics, and passing through fanciful wall openings from one space to the next, he finds architecture and ornamentation so cunningly joined with rockery and plantings as to blur the distinctions that normally separate one from the other. The visit unfolds as an immersion in a landscape of nature and art that satisfies both the sensual and intellectual appetites. At the same time, the spiritual content of a Chinese garden emanates from its land-forms and rocks, presented as metaphors that subtly suggest the sublimity and timelessness of the scenic grandeurs of the world outside its walls.

Far from being a fevered vision seen in a dream, the classical garden so described may still be experienced. Though formerly the private property of members of the upper ranks of Chinese society — rulers, nobility, scholars, artists, merchants and landowners — the gardens today are cared for under the stewardship of Chinese cultural authorities. Virtually all of them were built during the Ming and the Qing dynasties, and although they have undergone many alterations and renovations, they remain as survivors of a unique art form dating back to Han times, almost 2,000 years ago.

As first conceived, the Chinese garden was a vast pleasure park containing plains, hills and valleys, streams, lakes and islands. Trees,

shrubs and flowers of many species filled its woods and fields, which were used both for hunting and outings by members of the imperial court. A simple expression of nature, the garden-park was hardly distinguishable from the wild landscape outside its confines.

In later periods interest in the natural landscape spread beyond the court to lower officialdom, religious institutions and the *literati*. Much more modest in scale, their gardens served as a setting for domestic life, and also provided space for a tranquil retreat reserved for quiet introspection. Both the salutary effects of solitude, as well as the elevation of the spirit in contemplation of abstractions of distant landscapes, were sought. Man's innate yearning for close contact with nature was clearly recognised and accommodated. This ideal is expressed in the often recurring theme in paintings which depicts the recluse, the hermit-philosopher, meditating within a remote and deep mountain fastness, far from the distractions of civilisation.

Thus motivated by their desire to be reminded of their country's remote natural landscapes, Chinese garden builders learned to produce in the reduced scale of gardens the effects of vast land forms. These were not vain attempts at imperfect realism — which could result only in mindless and vulgar imitation — but rather they were stylised versions of nature, subtle plays in symbolism. Within their gardens were placed features that evoked aspects of the wild: hills and mountains, convoluted and craggy rocks, waterfalls, streams, ponds, twisting paths and picturesque trees that showed the ageing effects of wind and time. Regular contact with these garden landscapes, it was hoped, would impart a deeper understanding of life.

Figure 1.1: 'The Gazing Garden: View of a Garden Villa', (section of a handscroll), Yuan Jiang, active c. 1690-1746. The Metropolitan Museum of Art, Gift of Constance Tang Fong, in honour of Mrs P.Y. Tang, 1982.

Figure 1.2: Nature in the form of rocks, water and trees pushes into the architecture while an artifact, like the stone stupa, emerges from the water. Zhuo Zheng Yuan, Suzhou.

Figure 1.3: To get adequate light into the courtyard the saplings are kept drastically pruned, leaving only a minimum of thin, airy branches and foliage. In this way plants cannot overwhelm the architectural framework. A low bamboo fence screens the landscape beyond the gate. The tablet reads: 'De Qi Huan Zhong (Find It Within the Circle)'. Shi Zi Lin, Suzhou.

And while perceiving the strong human affinity for nature, the Chinese also recognised man's appreciation of art. It was distinct from the pure emotion evoked by aspects of nature. In a garden, however, it was possible to cater to both of these human traits: the deep feelings aroused from contact with natural elements of the earth, and the intellectual response to a work of art.

The classical Chinese garden, then, formed within a predominantly architectural framework of walls and buildings is, in a sense, a multi-dimensional painting in space and time. As in nature, land features are arranged irregularly and asymmetrically. There are zigzags and curves. Objects appear gradually as one wanders from place to place. But even where the parts of the design show neither reason nor formula, there is neither disorder nor confusion. While the garden designer sees with the eyes of a painter in visualising nature's landscapes, he calculates as an architect. He bows to the logic and order of the demands of construction as well as to such intuitive concepts as *shan-shui*, the combining of mountains and water in a garden — an expression of *yin* and *yang*, the Taoist view of the balancing of opposites, the harmony and duality pervading all things.

Figure 1.4: Such a tai-hu *rock often can seem as insubstantial as a cloud ready to drift away over the garden wall or to dissolve into wisps that will disappear through the wall's grillework. Wang Shi Yuan, Suzhou.*

Although, in the abstract, the differences between nature and art may seem as irreconcilable as between emotion and reason, the contradictions within a Chinese garden are more apparent than real. Even in palace gardens, where the overall layout may be vast and grandiose, there is an intimacy within its parts and subdivisions. Individual features, as in a commoner's domestic garden, are on a scale there that is neither magnified nor dwarfed. Rather than engendering feelings of loneliness or awe, such gardens offer a choice of intimate retreats which are either inviting for a convivial party of friends or conducive to solitary meditation.

Thus the Chinese garden is to be experienced. One must physically move through its spaces, for only a hint of what lies around the corner is revealed from any one point. It is indeed a sharp contrast with the Zen temple gardens of Japan, whose spare and level terrains are experienced by observation from a window or porch. (A common characteristic of both, however, is that neither provides ground for exertive activities or the assembly of large groups of people.)

And in contrast with Western gardens, the Chinese garden is not essentially of horticultural interest, with a profusion of plants growing in wild abandon. Nor are there smothering thickets of overgrown shrubs and hedges. While both evergreen and deciduous trees and shrubs are planted in naturalistic arrangements — alone in pure stands, or in association with rocks — their growth, for the most part, is kept under control. Grasses may be planted among rocks or along shorelines of ponds and streams, but never as lawn. The ground is either covered with pavements and paths of stone, pebbles, or tiles, or simply exposed as clean, swept earth, interspersed with patches of moss or other low groundcovers. Sparse plantings of seasonal flowers are scattered here and there, as in wild nature (and never in geo-

Figure 1.5: What do you do with a courtyard in the shape of an irregular polygon, surrounded on three sides by a sheltered gallery which is a passageway for pedestrian traffic between building and courtyards? You can fill it with plants, or, following the Chinese practice of using features that stimulate fantasy and imagination, you can place tai-hu rocks there. They function on several levels: As forms of abstract sculpture viewed from three sides, they can be appreciated as the activators of purely intellectual exercise. Or, architecturally, they robustly subdivide the space, and consequently simply create the illusion of a larger space. And on the level of emotion and imagination, the rocks become friends and familiar companions for those who pass their way. For them they are craggy peaks in remote mountains, or the rocks may assume the characters of animals or even those of mythical sages of yore. The result is, of course, that whenever one passes by the experience lasts not merely the thirty seconds it takes to go a distance of twenty paces, but rather a measureless interval in time and space. Such is the effect which the Chinese garden creates over and over again: that reverberation between the reality of the material and the boundlessness of the imagination. With such evocative powers, little else is needed in the space except for the crape myrtle trees and ground covers of mondo grass and pavements of mosaics and stone chips and bricks with tile shards set on edge in a setting bed of clay and sand. Yi Yuan, Suzhou.

metric patterns), or are grown in pots and tubs that are shifted as they come into their blooming seasons. In this way, through control of the growth of plantings, and the garden's very architectural structure — weighty but not crushing — the garden is spared the character of a wild jungle.

It is rockery, however, that acts as the intermediary, transitional link between elements of pure nature, such as plants, and the garden's architecture. Rocks are valued for their bizarrerie of shape and for their capacity to suggest remote and mythical places. Often they are set simply against plain backgrounds, such as white, beige or grey walls, with little or no softening accompaniment of trees and shrubs, so that full appraisal may be made of their stark forms, jagged peaks, ridges and clefts, and the weird honeycomb of their cavities. These rocks, called *Tai-hu* rocks after the name of the lake where they are found, are of porous limestone that has undergone hydraulic transformation. They are perceived by the Chinese connoisseur sometimes as frozen music or as the terrestrial roots of heaven. Though rock-hard, they appear as ephemeral forms of the summer clouds that hover overhead and slowly drift across the sky, merging finally at the horizon into the transient mists of morning and evening.

In sum, the garden is an expression of the ideal accord of man and nature represented in the deft combining of the order and formalism of architecture with the irregularity and asymmetry of plants and rocks in stylised naturalistic arrangements. It must not be considered,

Figure 1.6: In this courtyard, no matter how imposing the rockery, the weight of the architecture reduces the rocks to a less than equal status. As a result, the natural elements — rocks, trees and other plants — play a subordinate role. Nevertheless, because of their close proximity to the residents of the house, they fulfil their other role of stirring up images of distant mountains and fantastic animals. Shi Zi Lin, Suzhou.

Figure 1.7: Rocks, like sculptural works of art, are introduced as close as possible to the building. The fantastic abstractions of their forms stimulate the imaginations of those inside, who see in them both distant landscapes as well as biomorphic forms. Modest in bulk, the rocks still play a powerful role in mediating the weight of the architecture around them. The largest rock to the left, while at first appearing top heavy, soon seems in perfect balance. Liu Yuan, Suzhou.

Figure 1.8: Through vase-shaped doorways, the scene in the background appears further away because it is seen through a space containing both light and shadow. Yu Yuan, Shanghai.

Figure 1.9: The garden wall effectively partitions off the courtyard providing the privacy necessary for the families on both sides. The wavy profile relieves the wall's overpowering mass, and, at the same time, can evoke images of a distant range of hills. This is especially true on misty days when only the faint outline of the wall is visible. The fringes of mondo grass around the rocks in the foreground serve as skirts to hide the rocks' junction with the ground and stone pavement. Plants in this view are peonies in the raised bed; loquat, banana and pauwlownia trees elsewhere. Yi Yuan, Suzhou.

Figure 1.10: Dividing passageways between courtyards into a succession of large and small spaces with narrowed-down openings exaggerates the perception of space and time as one moves through them. Liu Yuan, Suzhou.

however, as a mere decorative adjunct of the house, but rather as a natural extension of its rooms, serving to relieve and redress the restrictive formalism within the house. The garden becomes a refuge, a place of escape for finding simple joys, for release of passions where one can be spontaneous in expressing feelings. It has been said that inside the house man is Confucian: formal, dutiful, restrained, inhibited. Outside, in the garden, he is Taoist: carefree, newborn, primitivistic, romantic. There, man and nature become one.

Still, one may accept the Chinese classical garden on its native ground, as an embodiment of a particular way of life, and yet question the pertinence of such a detached and ancient art form in the life of contemporary Western man (and indeed in any modern industrialised society, East or West, which is soon to enter the twenty-first century). The hesitation is justified, considering the ages when the Chinese garden was widely presumed by outsiders to be primarily a strange and exotic artifice, the exclusive province of the elite, dilettantes, sinologues and dreamers. Today's compelling truth, however, is that this product of centuries reveals itself as a remarkably practical construction providing a down-to-earth mechanism for living in crowded urban settings. Although the original genius of this unique synthesis of natural and man-made forms is, of course, remote

in distance and time, the lessons it can teach remain as fresh as ever. The world has much to gain in learning its design principles and land planning techniques.

What then are the bases of those arcane principles and techniques that make the classical garden so successful and so worthwhile an object of study and application? Some are grounded in China's indigenous philosophies and religions; others derive from limitations of space and the requirements of an economy of function developed through the 5,000 years of history and human experience of a pragmatic culture with a timeless capacity for renewal. But aside from the practical geometry of its spaces, or its surface exoticism and picturesque style, the Chinese garden, transcending its distinctive forms, reflects simply a profound understanding of the workings of the human mind, of the things that move a man.

Today such considerations of the human response to the physical landscape are pertinent because they bear directly upon the ever-growing sense of alienation among people in highly developed industrialised societies. Although such urban disaffection stems from a myriad of historical and sociological roots, it is unhappily intensified when the urban environment's links with nature are severed. The resulting sterile, unevocative landscape, which has lost touch with almost all aspects of the natural, strikes urban man cold. It leaves him unmoved. There are, however, antidotes to help relieve this pervasive numbness. That is why, at this time, the Chinese garden merits the attention of designers in the West. It offers an adaptable formula for restoring urban man's links with nature. An indication of the profound significance of that connection is shown by two paradoxes in the allegory of man in the Garden of Eden. The first: primitive man, living on his narrow niche in a nourishing though rude and strenuous paradise, begins to erode that pure state of nature as soon as he starts to develop his technology. The very forces that convert the dumb creature into a self-conscious human being cause his expulsion from that figurative Eden. At that moment, in order to survive as man, he begins to disrupt, in little ways at first, that finely balanced ecology that nurtured him from his beginnings. Soon the

Figure 1.11: Three panels from a handscroll painting: 'Purification At The Orchid Pavilion' by Fan I (early Qing). Courtesy of The Cleveland Museum of Art. Gift of the Junior Council of the Cleveland Museum of Art and of Mrs Wai-Kam Ho in the name of the Junior Council.

Figure 1.12: Roofed walkways and pavilions set in the midst of rockeries and plantings all make contact with nature a painless, comfortable yet intimate and immediate experience. This does not mean that all paths and routes, and vantage points are roofed over. But enough cover is provided so that at any time one may venture forth despite inclement weather to observe and experience some aspect of nature close up. From the protected interior of a loggia or gallery or a covered walkway lang, the wanderer may see rain pelting leaves and branches, dripping from rocks, wetting pebbled pavements or making concentric circles on the surface of ponds. Or, he may listen to the hissing of wind-driven snow and sleet falling on pine boughs or bamboo groves, or, in late winter, gently dabbing the blossoms and buds of camellia and plum. And at night the moon and stars may be comfortably viewed from kiosks (ting) and verandas. Zhuo Zheng Yuan, Suzhou.

Garden of Eden recedes farther and farther into an unremembered past. But man is fruitful and multiplies. He builds cities and becomes urban man. Civilisations rise and fall, and natural environmental systems deteriorate at an even faster pace.

Then, the second paradox: though he no longer lives in naïve concord with his originally natural world, man feels always the nostalgia to recapture it. Despite resigned acceptance that such long-ings are hopeless, that the journey is irreversible, that Eden is forever lost, he attempts, as if by instinct, often in modest ways, and some-times on a grand and elaborate scale, to hold on to symbols, some essence of that distant past: a plant in a flowerpot on a windowsill, a touching patch of green in a city backyard, a suburban garden or a park. Each in its way illustrates the act of man reaching back to his origins.

The metaphor of Eden seems clear when one examines man's first roots in the forest, and his later emergence on to the plain as a hunt-ing and territorial presence. He begins life well-equipped with a genetic legacy fused into every cell of his body. Departure from the womb signals merely the start of the process of acculturation, for at the moment of birth he is already richly endowed with an array of primordial instincts, impulses, longings and adaptive responses, built in through countless generations of selection.

Referring in *So Human An Animal* to this indissoluble link with the past, biologist René Dubos wrote:

The inner life of modern man is still influenced by very ancient biological processes that have not changed since Paleolithic times, and of which he is often completely unaware . . . It is dangerous to

Figure 1.13: Sheltered passageways and galleries serve as all-weather links between buildings within a garden compound. Projecting from the water, the carved stone Buddhist stupa is not merely a focal point of interest as an antique work of art, but, more importantly, acts as a turning point for the viewer moving down the gallery. The more distant landscape beyond seems to revolve around the pivot of the object in the water. Zhuo Zheng Yuan, Suzhou.

yield without thought to the call of the wild, but perhaps destructive to ignore it altogether. While the voices of the deep may seem strange, and at times frightening, they are the expressions of forces that must be reckoned with, because they are inherent in the human race and influential in all aspects of human behavior.

And so modern man appears on the scene, already programmed, carrying that inheritance for all time.

Evidence of its existence is supported by scientific research. One study of Iltis, Loucks and Andrews, for example, discovered that

> mental health and emotional stability of populations may be profoundly influenced by frustrating aspects of an urban, biologically artificial environment . . . It seems likely that we are genetically programmed to a natural habitat of clean air and a varied green landscape, like any other mammal.

The planner, Pierre Schneider, writes about this human dependence:

> Cities teach us history and progress. Nature reminds us of the timeless, of what in us has not changed any more than trees, the sky or the light of day. The desperate rush into the countryside that jams French roads every weekend [indeed the roads of all of Western Europe and America as well] indicates that history does not answer our needs.

In effect, no anthropological theory need be offered in order to

Figure 1.14: Three panels of a handscroll painting: 'The Garden For Self-enjoyment' by Qiu Ying (active c. 1522-1560). Courtesy of The Cleveland Museum of Art Purchase, John L. Severance Fund.

accept one simple truth, based, in a real sense, on the observable data of actual experience: in our own lives we find that contact with nature, or, failing that, even with symbols of aspects of nature transplanted from wild or rural areas into urban environments, work salutary effects upon the human spirit. What we find in nature is ourselves. It is a part of ourselves that is increasingly difficult to find in cities: the cycles of the seasons, the faithful rhythms of nature, its quiet truths.

Genetics and natural selection may thus explain the simple reaching out of the human species to nature. But inevitably we are led to examine the composition and quality of those instincts and impulses.

The clearest expression of those built-in responses may be found in man's emotions. It is, after all, emotion coupled with intellect that distinguishes a man. Intellect has led him often to reject nature as he found it by attempting to master it; emotion has led him to embrace it. His concern now is to use his intellectual powers to preserve and enhance his natural environment for reasons of his very survival, and in the process, to respond to his instinctive identification with that legacy that always remains within him.

And so what we have come to realise now, the Chinese have known for centuries: how to benefit from the emotive potentialities of nature's landscapes. They are uniquely sensitive to all its forces. Yet although all early cultures developed in circumstances that were subject to the same full range of natural forces which had to be dealt with, explained, adapted to, tamed, channelled, propitiated, utilised and defended against, from earliest times it was China, on the remote eastern flank of Asia, conditioned by all the physical resources and climates of its peculiar geography, which developed the creative empathy with nature that so deeply permeates every aspect of its arts and technology. That characteristic feeling, eloquently reflected in the works of poets and painters, also became the major influence in the design of their gardens. And between poetry, painting and garden ebbs and flows such a lively interplay of cause and effect that often each seems simply to be an aspect of one single, all-embracing art form. There are gardens, for example, inspired by poetry and painting; poetry inspired by painting and gardens; and painting inspired by gardens and poetry. Thus, strolling in a garden, one encounters tablets of wood and stone, incised in cursive-style calligraphy with verse evoking the lyrical mood of a particular part of the landscape. Or, in another part of the garden one may find a rock grouping with a waterfall and gnarled pine or plum tree, interpreting an evocative scene from a painting by an artist of renown in an earlier century. In each instance, however, though the bounds and framework of a garden may be architectural, the features with the emotion-stimulating, poetic content are composed of such natural elements as hills, valleys, rocks, streams, ponds, islands, groves of trees, and flowers, always reminding the viewer of the larger landscapes lying outside the garden's man-made limits.

Still, having perceived in a garden the priority of features of nature, the Chinese also recognized that works of man, under certain conditions, when transmuted by the forces of nature to show the mellowing effects of time and weather, have the power to stir the emotions. Consequently, they welcomed bleaching of wood in sunlight, darkening of stones and masonry, patina formation on bronze and copper, rust on iron, lichens on stone, moss between pavers, plant growth that changes the relative scale of an artifact in the landscape, erosive action of water on rock slabs, limestone accretions, scouring action of snow and ice, freezing and thawing, the play of sunlight and moonlight on the swept ground of a courtyard, shadows of trees on walls, the smoothing and wearing down of stone pavements by the traffic of feet over many years, wetting of rain on

Figure 1.15: In autumn the courtyard's falling leaves evoke a misty tone of melancholy. Yet the crisp lines of eaves and walls hold it all in a solid embrace. On foggy days the walls disappear. Liu Yuan, Suzhou.

Figure 1.16: Architecture facing nature eyeball to eyeball. The rockery cliffs and plantings at water's edge evoke far-off mountain lakes. Yi Yuan, Suzhou.

stone, the fading of pigments, the creaking of a water wheel, and the accumulation of knobs on a tree after many seasons of pruning. Thus, the action of time, weather and living organisms upon the works of man, as well as upon those of nature, works its changes, and thereby seems to improve them.

What then is the essential quality assumed by a garden that converts it into a moving, emotion-producing work of art? It is simply the capacity to offer metaphors and illusions of nature, and to be transformed by nature, to assume a new life and, through weathering, to give back part of its substance, and with it to become a link in the larger mesh of life.

In the final analysis, the true test of a garden's success, by Chinese standards, is to judge it according to whether or not it satisfies the expectation that something is happening, or that something *has* happened, that a process is continuing or has been completed, and that time is passing or has passed.

Figure 1.17: The sharply defined dark frame of the 'moon gate' provides the bracing contrast with the light, unstructured elements of the natural landscape beyond. It encompasses it all in a circular frame, as in a painting. Zhuo Zheng Yuan, Suzhou.

Chapter 2
Chinese Gardens and Japanese Gardens: Affinities and Contrasts

The three hundred years of the Tang Dynasty (618-907 AD) brought gardens, along with other arts, to new levels of refinement and sophistication. Word of these innovations in styles of architecture and landscape art inevitably reached Japan, where they were enthusiastically adopted by the imperial court. So lasting was the effect of those early contacts that even into the present day Japanese gardens show evidence of origins deeply rooted in Tang China.

Yet, despite the common heritage, garden design in the two countries developed from earliest times along separate lines. Their arts found nourishment in different soils and climates among peoples of dissimilar race, culture and history. Today the differences between Chinese and Japanese gardens, overriding their affinities, place them in clearly separate worlds.

To understand where the two garden traditions diverge, consider first the common ground from which they emerged, and the fundamental beliefs and traditions shared by the two peoples. Through the centuries most self-evident is their reverential deference to nature, whose all-embracing concept (in China called *zi-ran*; in Japan *shizen*) is denoted by the two-character word composed of the ideograms for 'self' and for 'being' or 'essence'. This compound word represents the sum and substance of creation, without reference to a first cause but simply as spontaneous fact. Man, then, stands as one element, albeit the most complex, in the intricate web of nature and life. And all natural phenomena become his eternal companions, to be appeased when required, and, ultimately, to be adjusted to. In both China and Japan men have learned to live with those forces beyond their control as part of the compelling reality of existence.

Such is a metaphysics where man holds no place as lord of Creation. Though he may be first among equals — the most notable of the Ten Thousand Things (as objects and creatures of nature are called in Chinese cosmogony) — as one of them his greater satisfaction is found in communion with nature's other beings, both sentient and inanimate, whom he regards as his brothers. It is a tenet that still prevails in many pantheistic cultures. Acceptance of the need to submerge one's being into the endless cycle of birth, growth, decline and death was imprinted upon Chinese and Japanese psyches — both under the transforming spell of Taoism.

Taoism, the philosophical system propounded by Laozi and his follower Chuangzi in the 6th century BC, dealt with the relationship of man to nature, and with the very ontology of Creation itself. Its effect upon Asian life and aesthetics was described by Okakura Kakuzo, the late-19th-century Japanese teacher and critic, in his *Book of Tea*:

> Chinese historians have always spoken of Taoism as the 'art of being in the world', for it deals with the present — ourselves. It is in us that God meets nature, and yesterday parts from tomorrow ... The art of life lies in a constant readjustment to our surroundings. Taoism accepts the mundane, as it is, and, unlike the Confucians and Buddhists, tries to find beauty in our world of woe and

worry. The Sung allegory of the *Three Vinegar Tasters* explains admirably the trend of the three doctrines. Sakyamuni, Confucius and Laozi once stood before a jar of vinegar — the emblem of life. Each dipped his finger in to taste the brew. The matter-of-fact Confucius found it sour, the Buddha called it bitter; and Laozi pronounced it sweet.

Then, indicating how Taoism illustrates the value of suggestion in art, Okakura reminded the beholder that in leaving something unsaid, he is given

... a chance to complete the idea, and thus a great masterpiece irresistibly rivets his attention until he seems to become actually a part of it. A vacuum is there for him to enter and fill up to the measure of his aesthetic emotion.

Finally, Okakura showed how Taoism was the strongest force behind the later development of Zen, the least structured and most individualistic of all the sects of Buddhism.

Contrasting it with Confucian classicism, Taoism's influence was characterized by the writer Lin Yutang as the romantic school of Chinese philosophy:

First, it stands for the return to nature and romantic escape from the world, and revolt against the artificiality and responsibilities of Confucian culture. Second, it stands for the rural ideal of life, art

Figure 2.1: A kare-san-sui garden for meditation at a Zen temple. The groundcovers are moss and shirakawazuna (particles of decomposed granite). Daitokuji, Kyoto, Japan.

Figure 2.2: The high wall enclosing a section of courtyard seems lower and less finite because windows have been placed at eye level. The garden-viewer does not have to peer through the opening in the wall to lose the feeling of confinement. The grillework, in the cracked ice pattern, permits just the right amount of visual penetration to offer hints of what lies on the other side. The ultimate effect is of a much larger space. Setting the windows aslant demonstrates how the rules may be broken to suit the designer's plan. They remind the viewer of two eyes gazing into other parts of the garden. Wang Shi Yuan, Suzhou.

and literature, and the worship of primitive simplicity. And third, it stands for the world of fancy and wonder . . .

Similarly, the Taoist concepts of man's relationship to nature are described in an analysis of Chinese painting:

. . . The voidness of the non-void is hinted at by vague expanses of ocean, snow, cloud and mist, and by solid objects which seem just on the point of emerging from, or melting into, the void. Man's triviality in relation to heaven's vastness is suggested by rolling landscapes in which mortals and dwellings appear insignificant against the grandeur of their surroundings. Mountains appear cloudlike; clouds resemble mountains; rocks and tree trunks seem strangely animated, as though they were peering at the viewer smiling; or the contours of men and animals are so united with those of natural objects that they appear to be of a single substance. Apparently, trivial objects — say a dragonfly perching on a twig — arouse a sudden intuition that each tiny creature is a particularization of a vast and holy universality, an embodiment of

Figure 2.3: Granite Buddhist figures in a bamboo grove. Hakushasonso, Kyoto, Japan.

the inconceivable immensity of the Tao. Everything seems imbued with a portentous mystery on the very point of being unveiled; an eerie feeling is aroused that everything in nature is vibrantly alive ... The Taoist artist deliberately leaves his work unfinished, that the viewer may complete it from his own intuition. Just as in Zen, an apparently nonsensical set of words or sudden action may bring about an extraordinary communication from mind to mind, so do paintings of this kind sometimes cause an illuminating blaze of intuition to leap into the beholder's mind, and he is conscious of being touched by the flow of cosmic energy communicated by the painting.[1]

Buddhism only reinforced this karmic view of the world. First, in China, Buddhism took its place along with the already established systems of Taoism and Confucianism. Later, in Japan it flourished. Its more universalistic religious appeal provided a deeper spiritual foundation. Throughout East Asia it found eager adherents, for it infused the lives of pious followers with an aura of faith and devotion lacking in shamanistic animism and ancestor worship.

Figure 2.4: Mosaic pavement of pebbles in the cracked ice pattern. The dividers may be tile, brick, shingle or stone strips set on edge. The pebbles range in length from 1 to 2½ inches. The divider strips are ¾ to 1 inch wide. The pebbles and divider strips are set in a matrix of sand, clay, soil and cement. Wang Shi Yuan, Suzhou.

Figure 2.5: The butterfly and flower mosaics are of stone chips, pebbles, and ceramic shards set on edge. The surrounding pavement is brick. Yi Yuan, Suzhou.

Buddhism pointed the way to salvation while opening up the prospect of a boundless universe. Thus, Japan, though an island nation isolated from the mainland of Asia, came rapidly under the influence of cultural advances issuing from its more sophisticated continental neighbour, whose earlier development had been spurred and coloured by long contact with the other burgeoning centres of civilisation farther to the west.

Yet, co-existing with Buddhism, in both China and Japan, unculti-vated nature still remained for all peoples the abode of the old, unrelinquished gods, who would still serve as guides and inter-mediaries leading men to more intimate contact with the primary forces of the universe. Only in wild nature was to be found the neces-sary solitude, where one could seek communion with the source of nature's powers — and with one's self. The vast and sublime land-scapes of nature — mountains, valleys, rivers — became the ultimate refuge, the place of escape from the world, where man could attain self-realisation and even enlightenment. A typical expression of that yearning was voiced by the poet of the Tang Dynasty, Li Bo, in his verse, 'Questions and Answer Among The Mountains':

You ask me why I dwell in the green mountain:
I smile and make no reply, for my heart is free of care.
As the peach blossom flows downstream, and is gone into the unknown,
I have a world apart that is not among men.

In a similar vein, 800 years later, Li Jihua (1565-1635) described the spiritual indoctrination of a painter:

Huang Zizhu often sits the whole day in the company of bamboos, trees, brushwood and piles of rocks in the wild mountain, and seems to have lost himself in his surroundings in a manner puzzling to others. Sometimes he goes to the place where the river joins the sea to look at the currents and waves, and he remains there, oblivious of wind and rain, and the howling water spirits.[2]

In Japan, three centuries earlier, during the turbulent Kamakura Period, many Buddhist priests, especially those in the Zen sects, following the example of Chinese hermits and recluse priests, also renounced the world. Retiring to the mountains, they led lives of solitude and contemplation, far from scenes of war and civil strife. Like Li Bo, the Japanese poet Saigyo sang of the beneficent natural environment of mountains in his verse:

Deep amid the hills,
Let me sip the pure water
Of clear mountain rills
While gathering chestnuts where
They are fallen here and there.[3]

During Japan's frequently recurring periods of fighting and political turmoil, it was poets such as Saigyo and other Buddhist clerics who alone remained conservators of learning and science. When peace finally came, the example of their austere and unaffected way of life exerted a steady and profound influence on artistic taste, architecture, garden design, and especially the gardens and pavilions used for the tea ceremony.

But from earliest times in both China and Japan, no matter how determinedly one resolved to get away to the mountains, it was only the exceptional man who, in fact, could escape the lowlands of daily existence — throwing off the constraints and obligations of a worldly life — to achieve that much sought-after transcendence. Consequently, in order even to approach that ideal state, without abandoning everything and running away to embrace nature in the raw, a substitute was devised that permitted conduct of one's daily mundane activities while at the same time providing the setting — the landscape — where it was possible, at least to fantasise, that, in fact, one had escaped to the distant mountains. Gardens became the refuge.

In a garden both Chinese and Japanese man recreated nature in abstraction, evoking the vaster landscapes of the world outside the garden wall. It was in the stroll gardens of members of the courts where that re-creation of nature found its fullest scope, where were formed in reduced scale all the basic features of the wild landscape: rocky peaks, hills, valleys, streams, waterfalls and ponds. Since water and rocks were the primary ingredients of the mountain landscapes of their dreams and yearnings, it followed that those same elements should play a key role in their gardens — water in all its flowing, falling and still forms, and rocks in which they fancied seeing features of nature at a far grander scale. Indeed, it is significant that even as early as the 7th century it was a prized rock which the Japanese Emperor Suiko received as a gift from the Emperor of China.

Most sought-after were rocks that showed the patina of time (in Japan the quality termed *sabi*), manifested by dark tones, moss and lichens on the surfaces of stone lanterns and water basins; or the ageing effects of wear and weathering on pavements, rust on iron, verdigris on copper and bronze, and storms on trees.

To complete the gardens, the living elements of trees and shrubs, grasses and flowers were planted in such artful arrangements as to convince even the most jaded viewer that, in fact, he had been transported to some distant, mythical place. Often, so exquisite were the gardens, they seemed unreal. Some were built to represent actual famous Chinese and Japanese seashore or mountain landscapes, particularly those described in poetry or depicted in antique paintings. Such evocative scenes conveyed the atmosphere of timelessness, while ephemeral time was marked by the changing of the seasons — first growth, coming into leaf, blooming, and then the falling of leaves. Thus, in both Chinese and Japanese gardens the sense of the infinite duration of eons, as well as the transitoriness of life, play upon the emotions.

In both lands, moreover, because of their dependence upon the solid structures of woody trees and shrubs and rocks, gardens maintain their basic forms throughout the year. The precise relationships of scale between plants and inanimate forms, such as rocks and man-made features, are controlled within the confines of the garden through constant attention to the requirements of timely pruning performed by painstaking and vigilant gardeners.

But enclosure of a garden did not inevitably shut it off from contact with the world outside, for wherever exterior landscapes, such as distant mountains, were visible from within, and judged to be especially evocative, both Chinese and Japanese garden builders planned their works so that the outside scenery might be viewed from inside the garden. It became 'borrowed' scenery (in Japan termed *shakkei*), a natural extension of the garden itself, and an integral part of the total composition.

Even within the garden, moreover, resort to a variety of optical strategems conveyed the sense of greater space and distance. For example, *sawari*, the Japanese term for the illusion of greater depth of field, was induced through the calculated placement of semi-transparent screens — copses of trees and shrubs, or a fence — between the viewer and more distant points in the garden. Then, while progressing from space to space in a garden, there was the added evocation of pictorial impressions — two-dimensional pictures composed so that the natural features, viewed through the framework of a window, door or gate, might be perceived as a detail from a landscape painting.

Thus the garden, both in China and Japan, though not a faithful copy of nature, became its subjective interpretation — more idealistic than realistic. Yet in both countries gardens continued to be inspired by the fervent desire for communion with all the myriad phenomena of nature — ideas suffused with the doctrines of Taoism and Buddhism. This almost visceral esteem, though shared by both peoples, underwent many modifications which, in turn, spawned new forms of artistic expression when transplanted from Chinese soil to Japan.

Architecture and garden design developed in a changed physical setting among a people of vastly different culture and psychology. In their gardens, nevertheless, they both resorted to manipulation of perspective by making distances seem farther than they actually were, using psychological tricks to play upon normal presumptions about things unseen, and by hiding the evidence of these stratagems.

The differences between the two traditions are apparent simply by observing the designs and layouts — the arrangement of spaces, emphasis and subordination of features, and the choice of materials and finishes. To appreciate those obvious distinctions, one must examine first the rationales that have influenced their ultimate form. And, even without delving deeply into their cultural histories, it is possible to discover reasons why the Japanese make gardens different from the Chinese. Through characterisation of the two garden traditions, those differences show up in sharp relief.

Upon entering a Chinese garden one sees at a glance that it provides, above all, a setting for daily life. It accommodates an almost complete array of activities for all ages, from the infant to the elderly, within the Chinese extended family. What is created is an enclosed, protected world, a physical expression of the overall concept of home and dwelling place. There, houses become intimately enmeshed with the walled courtyard (or series of courtyards) to form one unified domestic structure. In the garden courtyard mothers nurse babies, children play; adults may make love in secluded pavilions, entertain friends, drink wine, eat, write poetry, look at the moon, and commune with nature by observing rocks, water, plants, flowers, birds and insects. And grandparents, with few duties except to watch over children, may simply rest in a sheltered corner, finding cool shade in summer, and in winter the warmth of sunshine.

These very concrete and mundane uses reflect the Chinese down-to-earth, pragmatic and undoctrinaire view of a garden. While garden features symbolic of nature's sublime landscapes are designed to uplift the spirit, the garden visitor feels free also to express the more earthy side of his being — feelings and emotions (the irreligious Taoist influence) — without the stifling constraints of Confucian rules. It is completely worldly, and, with few inhibiting barriers, a realistic acceptance of human nature, far removed from the more abstract, anti-rational and idealistic Japanese idea of a garden.

Thus, Chinese gardens are made for the physical presence of man, while Japanese gardens are at their best when viewed without people. One very good reason, of course, is that the presence of people in a Japanese garden disrupts illusions of scale. (The two exceptions are the extensive stroll or series gardens, formerly private, which are now open to the public, and the *roji* garden through which one must pass before participating in the formal tea ceremony.)

Today the garden in Japan, no longer a setting for everyday activities or light-hearted pleasure as in Heian times (eighth to twelfth centuries), has become a traditional adjunct of the house, an honoured place set apart. Although it too is enclosed behind walls and fences, and the rooms of the house do open onto it, the garden has taken shape as a somewhat exalted creation, a thing to be looked upon and appreciated from the viewpoint of the house, rather than to be physically occupied. It is regarded as something fragile and precious, to be approached with serious intent, and indeed often with reverence, as if it were a religious experience. In fact, the evocation in a Japanese garden of that sense of spirituality, idealism and a highly disciplined asceticism, when carried to extremes, may often inhibit relaxed enjoyment of its naturalism. Happily, such sterile dogma and gravity, which some commentators have pinned on Japanese gardens, is dismissed by the cooler heads of artists and free-minded scholars, who acknowledge that heavenly imputations are an undeserved burden that inhibits deeper appreciation of its character. Such undue solemnity would be laughed at by Laozi, Chuangzi and the early Zen fathers.

Nevertheless, despite the Japanese tendency to exaggerate the garden's shadowy spiritual depths, there is no denying the overwhelming sense of compression, the search for the minimal, and the

Figure 2.6: Ornamental copings, mainly of ceramic tile, serve many purposes. In purely practical terms, they serve as a leak-proof topping to the wall's integrity. From the viewpoint of design, the coping adds the finishing touch, the capping, to a stark, bare wall. It draws attention away from the ground plane, with the implications that there is an existence beyond the earthly fabric of everyday life. And, both its geometrical form as well as its biomorphic symbols evoke myths, superstitions and mysticism. There is a paradox here. Although their strange, wild imagery can stir up flights of fancy, they are of the humblest of earthly material — clay. Yu Yuan, Shanghai, and temple garden, Nanjing.

Figure 2.7: The crinkled and pitted limestone shaft, frequently hidden by foliage around its lower part, reminds the viewer of a mountain peak thrusting its spire through the clouds — a theme frequently depicted in Chinese landscape paintings. Liu Yuan, Suzhou.

stripping away of the non-essential, so characteristic of the general Japanese approach to the arts. (In contrast, the more practical and materialistic Chinese, emphasising the explicit and the concrete, place less reliance on the viewer's imagination.) In the walled compounds of Japanese Zen temples one finds *kare-san-sui* compositions, the flat, dry garden of sparse rock arrangements, such as Ryoan-ji, set on a finely gravelled plain. From the *hojo* veranda the viewer gazes in quiet contemplation of the fifteen rocks and raked gravel spread before him. This abstraction of a landscape becomes, at that moment, a *mandala* often inducing a trance-like state, almost akin to that produced by a psychedelic substance. He sees oceans and islands where there are only rocks and raked gravel. Likewise, in the

Figure 2.8: Placed upright in front of a wall, a tai-hu rock is particularly appreciated when it is back-lighted so that its silhouette is sharply delineated as if it were a piece of sculpture. Aside from the pure aesthetics of its form, and the way in which it serves as a dominant design element in the total composition of rocks, wall and trees, it also evokes images and fantasies of those remote places that carry the beholder beyond the garden's walls. On the left stands a lacebark pine; on the right a podocarpus tree. Yu Yuan, Shanghai.

less formal setting of a house, the Japanese home-owner, even if the cost of introducing water into his garden is affordable, may, in any case, be quite contented with, and even proud of, his simulated dry stream. But if he insists on having water, he will be happy with the slow drip and trickle of water from a bamboo spout into a stone *chozubachi* or *tsukubai* water basin. In general, however, for the Japanese mind, the *idea* of water — its *abstraction* — is as satisfying as water itself. To imagine through a spurt of concentration that one actually *has* water is a Zen exercise that appeals to the Japanese temperament.

The Chinese, on the other hand, see in water far more than its surface charm. For them it is a clear symbol of the duality of the Tao:

'There is nothing softer and weaker than water, and yet there is nothing better for attacking hard and strong things. For this reason, there is no substitute for it.' So wrote Laozi.

The Chinese garden builder, moreover, has never resorted to exploitation of the imagination to the extent tried by his Japanese counterpart. In China, wherever it is economically feasible, water is introduced into a garden in the form of a pond or running stream. But where that is not possible, the substitute of a Japanese-style *kare-san-sui* garden is not even considered. One reason, of course, is the great value placed by the Chinese upon contact with water, particularly in the dry, dusty continental climate of the provinces north of the Yangtze River, where drought is an ever-present concern. In Japan, by contrast, with its generally abundant rainfall, where no part of its mountainous islands are very far from bodies of water, at every turn are encountered streams and rivers. No wonder then that the extensive use of water, though desirable, can be dispensed with if considerations of space or economy make it prohibitive. The Japanese owner of a *kare-san-sui* garden knows that he has only to step outside his garden, and in the space of a few minutes he can find a stream or trickling rill, alongside the road, or running into nearby rice paddies. For the practical Chinese, however, instead of laying out a finely gravelled flat stretch of terrain which it is forbidden to tread upon, it is far better to pave part of his walled garden courtyard, or simply to set aside a section of swept, packed earth for potted plants and for children's play. In contrast, the Japanese child learns early in life that the garden — his father's special province — is no place for games.

In short, to experience all the elements of a Chinese garden, one must live in it, move through it, physically occupy it. It has become a three-dimensional, personal, spatial experience with the added sense of periodic, diurnal and seasonal time. The domestic Japanese garden, on the other hand, generally can be grasped best from one or two restricted stations inside or close to the house. Even in larger stroll gardens, the viewer's freedom to roam is subtly controlled. He is confined to a path from which the views of the garden enfold in progression along a predetermined track. There are none of the paved or swept open spaces of Chinese courtyards where one can wander at will. And although in Chinese gardens certain views are composed to be seen enframed by doorways, gates and windows — in a sense, a two-dimensional picture similar to the view of an especially charming or picturesque segment of a Japanese garden seen through the open *shoji* of a *tatami* mat room — one still may stroll randomly around and through the paved open spaces of a Chinese courtyard to view the various features from whatever angle or range selected. Such choices do not exist in a Japanese garden. There one must respect the moss.

In addition to the very obvious characteristics of how a garden is physically used, in comparing Chinese and Japanese gardens more subtle distinctions merit examination. In a Chinese garden, for instance, because it is so much an integral part of the daily life of the users, one feels strongly the personality of the garden's creator. His intent may be judged by the balance he has made between naturalistic features and man-made elements; the division of space between planted areas and bare surfaces, and the choice of materials — in sum: the proportion of space reserved for physical function *vis à vis* purely aesthetic or spiritual purposes. Further, an even more explicit indicator of the 'intent' of the garden-maker is the use of tablets posted about the garden, incised with messages for the viewer of the moment, and for posterity. The writings on those stone or wood plaques range from mottoes, aphorisms, and poetic verse to historic allusions and quotations from sages and emperors. One may even judge from those selections the politics of the garden's builder — his leaning toward the liberalism of Laozi or the conservatism of Confucius.

In contrast, Japanese gardens are much more impersonal. Their statements of design offer no intermediary. The particular 'self' of the creator is transcended in its enigmatic abstractions, with only a few hints by which to judge him: one reason being the sometimes compliant adherence to design rules, thus allowing less freedom of expression to the designer. It is rare to find poetry tablets posted in the Japanese garden. Nor is the need felt to commemorate there important historical events.

The contrasts in the way the Chinese and Japanese think about their gardens, and the way they use them, is reflected, further, in every aspect of their designs. The presence of many man-made elements in a Chinese garden tend to impart a rococo feeling which Japanese garden builders try to avoid. A strong impression from Chinese gardens is of skilled artifice, a magical, and slightly fabulous landscape of dreams. One is struck at once by the choice of materials and finishes, by the tendency towards embellishment, intricate elaboration of surfaces, the repetition of themes that are developed and refined in pavements, copings, walls, gates, windows, lattice and grillework. Architectural detailing is ornate. There is a profusion of materials and colours. Wood is often painted. Architecture and artifacts seem to predominate over natural materials. But while rocks and plants may seem to play a lesser role, they are sensitively combined with, and interwoven into, the walls and pavements to form indissoluble compositions. Elaboration of architecture has existed from ancient times, but became overly ornate only in the later years of the Qing, the last dynasty which finally collapsed in 1912.

Nor was Japan immune from the tendency to embellish. The last years of the Tokugawa Shogunate, through the Meiji and Taisho periods, were a time of aping of Victorian and Edwardian extravagance. In gardens that tendency towards ornamentation was seen mainly in the design of excessively elaborated artifacts, such as stone and bronze lanterns. Aside from that relatively brief period of cultural anomaly, however, the Japanese have paid homage, and continue to do so, to the cult of plainness in their gardens and other arts. Simplicity and even austerity are admired. Opulence and over-decorated effect are avoided. Domestic architecture, and most religiou structures are plain, unadorned and unpainted. *Shoin* and *sukiya* tyles of dwelling design exemplify the insistent quest for natur ness and rusticity, even to the point of starkness. The emphasis is on form. Decoration plays only a minor role. This is not to imply, however, that the Japanese are not concerned with surfaces. It is only in the tone and texture where Chinese and Japanese tastes diverge. While both value an antique quality, the Japanese prize rougher surfaces and textures, less colour, bare, aged wood — *shibusa* (astringency) and *sabi* (signs of age and wear and tear). A clear illustration of those preferences may be seen in comparing the plain and neutral patterns and earth tones of *raku* pottery bowls used in *cha-no-yu* (the tea ceremony) with the soft elegance and refinement of a Sung *lungchuan* celadon bowl or *zhunyao* cup.

The Japanese preference for quiet design in architecture and gardens is shown also in limiting the variety of materials — for the most part, stone, wood, bamboo and plants. The predominant material, however, is plants. The non-growing element plays a minor role — the one exception being the Zen stone and gravel garden. The feeling, moreover, is that architecture (the Japanese house) and the garden are separate provinces. And although, at the point where they meet, very subtle transitions and blendings of the several materials do occur, there is nothing that equals the complete and irrevoc-

Figure 2.9: A Meiji Period stroll garden, formerly property of the Japanese imperial family; now open to the public. Shinjuku Gyoen, Tokyo.

able bonding of the Chinese garden courtyard and house.

The weight of architecture in a Chinese garden is further accentuated by the overwhelming preference for masonry — bricks, stone, pebbles, stucco, plaster, tile — in walls, pavements and gateways. Rarely are spaces partitioned by wood or bamboo fences. The masonry wall of a Chinese garden, an inseparable part of the whole design, is to keep outsiders from seeing in, while the enclosure of a Japanese garden is to prevent those inside from having to see out. Wherever possible, the Japanese de-emphasise the wall or fence, often hiding it, blending it in with the plantings, or placing it out of sight behind a hill.

In contrast with the Chinese use of solid and opaque enclosures, the Japanese divide up their interior garden spaces with aponogetonic screens — wood and bamboo fencing — permitting air and light to pass through. Space dividers within the garden are formed by these organic materials, and by growing plants in sheared hedges. In China such hedges are rare.

A further distinction in the landscape art of the two countries is sharply illustrated in the way rocks are used. Both use rocks in profusion as one vital element of garden scenery, symbolic of natural landscapes outside. But at that point the resemblance ends, for there could not be a greater divergence than in their use. This essential disparity applies not only to the type of rock material itself — its source, composition, texture, colour and shape — but also its handling, arrangement, placement, juxtaposition and interpretation.

The rocks of a Chinese garden are of two types: one, basaltic, of igneous origin, are solid boulders and angular rocks with a heavy, bulky feeling, and tan, beige and yellow in colour. This type is termed *huang-shitou*. The second, and more unique type are sedimentary — composed of a calcareous grey limestone plucked generally from the shores and bottoms of lakes, ponds and rivers. Their convoluted surfaces, often pierced, showing the effects of hydraulic forces, convey a plastic quality, as if the stony material were even malleable. In fact, man in China has often played an active role in the metamorphosis of many of the rocks destined for gardens, by dumping those with promising lineaments into lakes or under waterfalls where the action of the water will hasten the formation of the hollows and the weird honeycomb of their cavities. Rocks subjected to water action are known as *tai-hu* rocks, after the name of the great Lake Tai and West Lake at Hangzhou, from which they are frequently taken. *Huang-shitou* rocks and *tai-hu* rocks are never combined in the same rock grouping.

In placing the rocks in the garden, the Chinese garden builder may either put them together, deftly piling one on top of the other to form a rocky cliff of a mountain or hill or the rocky shoreline of a pond or lake; or he may create the effect of rock outcrops and ledges interspersed among plantings of trees and shrubs. The rocks are carefully pieced together to create the effect of giant formations. Pigmented mortar is cunningly used to hide the joints.

Whenever an unusually evocative rock is to be placed in a garden, its unique symbolic presence may require that it stand alone, often on a pedestal or plinth, like a work of monumental sculpture or stone stele, with the plain background of a white plaster wall. Eventually, such a free-standing rock may assume a life and personality of its own. It becomes a familiar character, a 'friend of the family', at times biomorphic — the mimetic image of a legendary deity, old man, lion or dragon. Vivid examples of such rocky creatures appear as the crouching and frolicking stone lions in the garden 'Shi-Zi-Lin' (Stone Lion Grove) in Suzhou.

Thus the rocks of a Chinese garden act as the intermediary, the transitional link between elements of pure nature, such as plants, and the garden's architecture. They are valued for their bizarrerie of shape and for their capacity to suggest remote and mythical places. They impart at once both the impression of the concrete solidity of matter as well as the feeling of the plasticity and mutability of things — an expression of a basic dichotomy within the Chinese view of life. The rocks become the corporeal embodiment of the dual forces of yin and yang in the Tao. Whenever the viewer looks upon the garden's rockery he is reminded of Laozi's teaching that the softest things in the world overcame the hardest. These Taoist symbols of the evanescence of life reach beyond their apparent surface grotesquerie with their power to evoke fantasy in the mind of the beholder.

In contrast with the Chinese metaphysical perception of rockery in a garden, the Japanese idealisation starts and finishes on a less fanciful level. The material itself is substantially different. While in China the typically prized tai-hu rock is sedimentary, in Japan the most sought-after garden rocks are the denser, heavier and harder metamorphic granites and cherts. Mountains, valleys, field, forests and shorelines may be the sources, but in all instances the rocks are simple, uncomplicated forms, solid in bulk, conveying a sense of permanence and stability. They are not pierced or contorted into weird shapes. If a Japanese rock is prized for the evocative power of its form, it is rarely a metaphysical concept or image that is sought; nor is it valued because it looks like an animal or person. Rather, it is valued for its evocative power to symbolise a common landscape feature — a hill, mountain, cliff, waterfall, or rocky islet. Aside from its simple, solid form, the characteristic most highly esteemed by the Japanese is the rock's finish — the texture, tone and colour of its surfaces The more signs of age the better. Instead of the cosmic Chinese allusions to heaven, the rocks in a Japanese garden, if anything, beyond their purely abstract form, symbolise the bare bones of the earth.

Even the manner of rock arrangements differs in the two countries. In Japan rarely are rocks piled up, one on top of the other, to form a rockery of ledges along a shoreline, or to simulate craggy cliffs. Nor are rock fragments pieced together and cemented with mortar. If a large rock must be split in order to facilitate handling, it will be reassembled carefully, as if it were unbroken, with the joints expertly concealed with vines, mosses and lichens. Often a choice rock may be particularly appreciated by the Japanese garden owner,

Figure 2.10: A natural feature in a garden, such as a tree or rock, may come to acquire a significance far different from its generally accepted designation. In fact, after a time it may become such a familiar landmark that the people who dwell there endow it with a unique personality of its own. How could the family which once lived here not regard this 'creature', the standing tai-hu rock, as Mr Otter, Mr Squirrel or Mr Marmot? It is a typical example of the Chinese precept: evoke fantasy in a garden, stir the imagination at every chance. Liu Yuan, Suzhou.

but unlike his Chinese counterpart, he desists from placing it on a pedestal standing clear of other features, almost as if it were an icon or idol awaiting adoration. For the Japanese, no matter how precious and rare the rock, it still must serve as one element of a larger grouping of rocks. All in all, the Japanese sees the stones in his garden as essential down-to-earth material. They provide the solidity, unchanging stability and sense of timelessness that balance the dynamism of growing plants. They are the fundamental element of inertia, calm and quietude that makes one feel in a garden that time is holding its breath.

Finally, in addition to rocks, plants in many respects are treated differently in the two garden traditions. As a rule, trees in both Chinese and Japanese gardens are used naturalistically, emphasising their structures and lines, with no attempt to impose on them geometric forms, or to make them serve the function of a topographic feature. Shrubs, on the other hand, in a Japanese garden may be used quite differently. They are often sheared into rounded shapes or simple blocks, as hedges, which become living architectural forms linking pure nature with man-made structures. Or, they may serve as symbolic elements — hills and mountain ranges — seen often in the sheared, mounded, undulating hillocks of azaleas and hollies. The flowers of sheared shrubs have little design significance as compared with the strongly defined, compact shape of the shrub itself.

In Chinese gardens, conversely, shrubs, like trees, are treated naturalistically; and though carefully pruned and thinned, they do not become substitutes for mass. There is so much bulk in the masonry walls, other architectural structures and rockery that plants are used mainly for line and colour in the overall garden design.

Pronounced disparities are evident as well in the treatment of the horizontal surfaces of the ground. In a Japanese garden the groundcovers may be a mix of grass, moss, low herbaceous or woody creeping plants, stone pavement, gravels, pebbles and stepping-stones. Rarely is the ground exposed without some covering — either growing or inanimate. But in the domestic Chinese garden the predominant groundcovers are pavings or swept earth whose bare stretches are interspersed with naturalised plantings of trees and shrubs. Along rocky shorelines and stone ledges grow patches of moss, grasses, vines and low herbaceous plants. Pavements are composed of brick, tile, and pebbles in a variety of shades forming mosaics of repeated geometric patterns as well as figures of animals and flowers. This figurative mosaic pavement never appears in Japanese gardens.

Even the particular ways in which flowers are used point up the differences in the two garden traditions. In Japan flowers play a minor role in gardens where, instead of colour, the stress is placed upon line, form and shading. The occasional spot of colour may be inserted here and there among rocks, or may appear in the few flowers that remain on azaleas after shearing, the brief flowering in the spring of trees and shrubs, a naturalised bed of iris or chrysanthemums, or the red berries of an ardisia, cotoneaster or viburnum. In every instance, however, these plants are closely integrated into the basic pervasive

Figure 2.11: Stucco garden wall with window aperture in the conventionalised form of a peach. The grillework showing peaches on their branches is of baked clay. Shi Zi Lin, Suzhou.

naturalism of the garden. In Chinese gardens, however, much more interest and attention is drawn to flowering plants. Besides the early-blooming trees and shrubs, colourful flowers and fruit are introduced in almost all seasons in pots and tubs which may be shifted after the flowers fade. In addition, raised planting beds, retained by rockery, are common elements in the design with seasonal perennials such as peonies, chrysanthemums and salvia.

Notes
1 *Taoism: The Road to Immortality* by John Blofeld.
2 *My Country And My People* by Lin Yutang.
3 Ibid.

Chapter 3
Planning and Practice

Playing with Illusion ... Applying Reality

In densely populated China every inch of usable land has had to serve some functional purpose, which, for a well-to-do family, meant, among its needs, construction of a classical landscape garden. It became, first, the integrating matrix that tied together the complex of buildings and courtyards accommodating an extended family clan and its retainers. At the same time the garden provided the means and the setting for stimulating constant appreciation of the many facets of its artistry among family members and friends. Finally, most uniquely, it exerted a peculiar therapy upon the minds and psyches of all those who came in contact with it. There, behind garden walls, the resident, as well as the occasional visitor, became isolated from everyday cares and burdens. As if transported to a far-off garden on the Mystic Isles of the Blest,[1] even brief contact with its myriad natural features instilled a sense of renewal. Such benefits made convincing proof that construction of a classical landscape garden was indeed a most economical and practical use of land.

How the garden worked as the integrating mechanism providing the means for easy communication between the various family sectors — while at the same time furnishing privacy and barriers between its components — is demonstrated in its complex layout of covered passageways (lang) and paths linking building to building. Beyond its purely functional design, however, the garden exerted its magic by inducing illusions that played with time and space, evoking a broad range of responses. The designers successfully appealed to the mind and heart because they understood the psychology of human perception and the realities of human needs.

Figure 3.1: Siting the building at the pond's edge permits its occupants to observe at close range the effect of weather on the water. In this instance, there is the fascination created by falling rain drops making ever-widening circles on the pond's surface. The jasmine plants along the far shore cascade down to the water. Wang Shi Yuan, Suzhou.

Form and Composition

From earliest times garden-builders were motivated by the desire to experience the pleasures of mountains, water, springs and forests, but without enduring the hardships of arduous journeys to remote places. The garden, therefore, had to furnish the sought-after secluded views of mountains and forest scenery. Every artifice of design was used — contrast, relief, projection, sequence, vista, 'borrowed scenery', scale — to achieve the illusion of natural landscapes in limited space. Gardens then became extensions and enlargements of the residence, with further elaboration of architecture. There were halls (*ting* and *tang*) for entertaining guests and receiving friends; courtyards as settings for daily life; stages for plays; studios for reading, writing and painting; and pavilions (*ting*), terraces (*tai*), storied pavilions (*lou* and *ge*) for resting and viewing the natural parts of the garden, where hills were piled up, ponds dug, and plantings made of trees, shrubs and flowers.

The simplest garden was the courtyard of a small residence. It was generally placed in front of or behind the main hall or study, and was embellished with rocks, plantings, a small pond and hills with adjacent porch or kiosk.

Figure 3.2: Just when the wanderer in the garden is surfeited with its bizarrerie and deviations, he comes upon this simple, narrow courtyard, symmetrically divided: two trees perfectly balanced with each other. The uncomplicated design expresses a formality and assurance, welcome antidotes to the asymmetry and meanderings of most of the garden. Only the bonsai pine in the pot on the centre pedestal has a mysterious implication that goes beyond its obvious placement. Over the doorway the tablet reads: 'Dong Shan Si Zhu (East Mountain Silk Bamboo)'. Liu Yuan, Suzhou.

Figure 3.3: The moon gate serves two functions: in the realm of artistic composition it captures the pond, the massed lotus, trees, bridge and pavilions simply by encompassing it all inside a circular frame, as in a painting. Its second function is to establish a correspondence with the moon gate in the distance while, through the substantial bulk of its construction, to equalise a balance between the garden's natural features and its architecture. Zhuo Zheng Yuan, Suzhou.

Medium-sized gardens, often an expansion of the smaller gardens, consisted of several minor courtyards surrounding the main space. Here the plan became more complex with the number of scenic features considerably increased. The medium- and larger-sized gardens often had several avenues of access: some with gates and openings in the outer wall leading directly from the street to permit viewing by the public and invited guests during certain festive occasions.

How Space is Divided Up

To gain the effect of a varied landscape in a limited area, the garden space is divided into separate scenic parts, each with its own distinctive character denoted by a particular feature, such as a pond, a tree, a hill, a rockery, or other landscape element. In laying out the garden and assigning to each sector its distinguishing feature, attention is paid to the order of importance of each element, as well as to the demands of comfortable and interesting circulation from one space to another. Where the hill and pond of a garden are designed as the main scenic sector, with subordinate spaces adjoining them, it is considered important to achieve the right balance between primary and secondary views. Thus, most well-designed gardens, because of the weight and importance of the distinctive character of their primary view, make a deep impression despite minor weaknesses elsewhere. For example, if a rockery hill grows dense bamboos or luxuriant flowering trees, its scenery becomes more prominent. On the other hand, if there are many hills, rockeries and ponds in a garden, none of which are outstanding, inevitably the whole garden will become fragmentary and centreless. The pond of one garden may be smaller than the pond of another. Yet it can seem more imposing and elegant if the features around its edges do not detract from the sheet of water, and also if it conveys the feeling of a confined space that does not 'leak away' around its edges. Consideration is given also to retaining a sense of openness and order.

At all times, of course, the main scenic feature must be integrated with the rest of the garden so that natural transitions are made from one sector to another. In Suzhou's classical gardens, where the primary sector is hill and water, subordinate parts may stress one or more particular species of flowering plants, a grove of bamboo, other water features, such as a stream or waterfall, a rocky peak, a single standing rock, or a pavilion. In each instance, the main subject differs, and its impact is affected by its immediately surrounding topography and the shape and heights of surrounding buildings.

Thus, to instill richness and beauty in the garden, some spaces should be large, others small; some open and bright, other closed and dark; some high, others low. Generally, one should pass through a space that is narrow, cramped and shady before entering a large scenic space. By first restraining and focussing down one's sights and

Figure 3.4: Long ago the Chinese decided that walls need not be straight, level, or uniform in height. Without a repeated module, masonry walls can assume any configuration. Stucco, cement, rubble, mud, adobe, and roof tiles adapt easily to an irregular linear flow, both laterally and vertically. Curved tops and moon gates are compatible with each other. Walls simply follow the undulating contours of the ground. Beyond the obvious symbolism of a dragon or reptile, meandering walls evoke the sense of a continuum of life — without beginning or end. There is a lack of finiteness, a refusal to conform to the demands of straight, square architecture. It is as if the Taoists were mocking the Confucianists. Meanwhile, it serves all the functions of a wall: separation of spaces, privacy, division of domain; yet it works in a way to express humour, a light heart, playfulness. As usual, the round aperture not only functions as outlet and escape hatch, but also frames the view of the scene beyond in a balanced and harmonious composition of plants and rocks. Yi Yuan, Suzhou.

Figure 3.5: Bamboo fence dividing service area from the rest of the garden. Xi Yuan, Suzhou.

sense of space, the sudden release into a light, open place makes one feel all the more carefree and joyous. With that end in mind, zigzag galleries, tortuous passageways, and small, secluded courtyards are first encountered after passing through the main gate as a prelude to reaching the garden's primary scenery.

Garden spaces are formed by walls, corridors, houses, rockery hills, groves of trees and bridges. To evoke a continual succession of emotional responses to each new space encountered, a varied mixture of both natural and architectural elements is employed to divide the spaces. In that way, hills and trees should alternate with walls, fences and buildings. In large gardens this is easily accomplished. In smaller gardens, however, spaces must be formed by walls, corridors and the sides of buildings. In order, therefore, to prevent the spaces from feeling too closed-in and partitioned, it is necessary to create gaps through which one can see, even if it is only a brief glimpse. Windows extend from floor to ceiling to allow indoor and outdoor space to run together. There should be many apertures: moon gates, latticed openings in walls, walls themselves built lower and with tops that undulate, and open pavilions and corridors with open sides.

Plant material also is used so that the trees and shrubs do not suffocate the space. Trees should be tall and high-limbed, shrubs sparsely branched and well pruned, and other shrubs and flowers dwarfed or prostrate. In that way sight lines are not obstructed nor space blocked up.

Garden Circulation and Directing the Spectator's View

To invite perception of the garden's scenic views, suitable routes of

Figure 3.6: Unglazed windows in a garden wall framed by mouldings of blackened terracotta. Dr Fu's Garden, Chengdu.

circulation are laid out. By carefully handling the relationship between points of interest and the spectator's route, features enfold themselves as if they were scenes from a continuous picture scroll.

Traditionally, the main hall (*ting* or *tang*) was the main focus of activity, and consequently, from it one faced the primary scenic feature of the garden — generally a pond with a hill on the far side. It was flanked by subordinate scenes composed of other rockeries, grottoes, smaller ponds, kiosks and plantings. The disposition of each point of interest depends on the topography — existing or man-made

Figure 3.7: The zigzag pattern of the bridge repeats the meanders of the paths that thread through the garden. Wandering over such indirect and complex routes, the visitor slows his pace, spending more time observing the plants and rocks, and consequently experiencing the illusion of wandering through a larger space. Yi Yuan, Suzhou.

Figure 3.8: Chiaroscuro: the Yang of bright, dynamic architecture, and the Yin of dark, receptive rockery. Liu Yuan, Suzhou.

— and the particular landscape character sought: open and bright, or secluded, tortuous and shady. High elevations along the spectator's route are located so that from them especially good borrowed views (if available) may be seen. Low points are placed to nestle up against a body of water so that the immediate landscape features are mirrored on its surface. The level of verandas and terraces built at the water's edge (so called 'land boats') is kept, if possible, lower than the surrounding grade. Heights of 'land boats' above water level may range from three feet to twelve feet, depending upon horizontal distances and the overall scale of the surrounding space.

In general, because of the limited area of the garden, the distance from the spectator's viewpoint and the scenic object is not long — from 40 to 115 feet. When it is the primary view, a rockery hill is usually no higher than 23 feet above the water level of the pond. If the distance from the spectator is too far, the rockery hill would look too low and small. A peak of *tai-hu* rock is better seen close up, surrounded by a plain background. As a rule, where the rocky peak is regarded as the main scenic object, its distance from the spectator is no greater than 65 feet. Besides the main vista, other scenes may be perceived from the main hall through side windows that frame each view.

The spectator's route itself must be varied in its topography, surface and surrounding features, with a mix of both architectural

Figure 3.9: By its very bulk, a covered bridge becomes an important landscape feature, not only on the land but also in the larger reflections it casts upon the water which it spans. It becomes, in any weather, a place for lingering while observing one's own reflection as well as the carp and goldfish that gather for feeding, and in the summer the plantings of lotus and waterlilies. In this instance, a roofed bridge provides continuous cover along the garden's major pathway and galleries as one moves within the garden from one place to another. The rockery along the shoreline is composed of basaltic 'yellow' rock. The shade trees are pines and camphors. Zhuo Zheng Yuan, Suzhou.

and naturalistic objects. Two types of paths are constructed. One demands less physical exertion as it follows obvious routes through buildings, corridors, zigzag covered galleries, courtyards and along the water's edge of garden ponds. The walking surfaces are easily negotiable, even for the elderly and the infirm. The second type, requiring a more adventuresome spirit and nimble feet, traverses narrow 'mountain' paths, coves, gullies, grottoes, hillside steps, gorges, defiles, and fords shallow streams and pools. Large gardens have enough space to contain both types of routes.

The simplest layout found in most gardens is the circular route. It encompasses the main hill and pond. From the main circuit branch off additional side paths that lead over the hill or across the water. Thus, the garden scenery can be enjoyed from a number of observation points and angles. Paths on hills are often made winding and tortuous to increase their lengths and to prolong the sightseeing experience. To economise on space, the outermost circuit is set as close as possible to the garden's border wall. It often forms one side of a long, meandering corridor, open on the garden side, and roofed to shield the garden wanderer from rain, snow and the direct rays of the sun. At the same time, this meandering, sheltered passageway serves the purpose of covering up the border wall. The various natural screening features located along the outside of the corridor — copses of trees, hills and rockeries — prevent the wanderer from taking

Figure 3.10: The clear view of open sky, repeated in the mirror of the pond, makes the garden — one of the smallest in Suzhou — seem larger than its half acre. The curved tree trunk on the left is a lacebark pine. The bridge is constructed of granite slabs. Wang Shi Yuan, Suzhou.

everything in at one glance. Thus, the route of travel through the garden spreads out everywhere, with constantly changing views: up into storied buildings and hills, down over bridges and across gullies, through open and closed places, offering distant views and sights at close-up, and looking from the outside into buildings, and from inside buildings to the outdoors.

Contrast, Dominance, Subordination

The impact of each garden feature is enhanced by studied consideration of its contrast with its background and the relationship between dominant and subordinate elements within each scene. In classical gardens there is constant play between denseness and sparseness, openness and walling-in of space, the refined craftsmanship of exquisite architectural details and the natural trees and rocks, and between the bright and the dark. If water is on one side of a rocky hill, then flowers and trees may be found on the other side. Relief is provided between courtyards and rockeries on the edges of a pond and the smooth, clear stretch of water in the middle. If one side of a body of water contains very naturalistic elements, such as rocks and trees, then on the opposite side may be placed architectural features.

In laying out the landscape, it is important to make clear what is

Figure 3.11: Here the contrast is reversed: the darker element is the wall and the scene beyond, while the gateway itself becomes the focus of brightness. The massiveness of the wall is balanced out by the powerful sinewy trunk of the old, gnarled tree. Temple of Heaven, Beijing.

primary and what is secondary. If the height of a hill is to be emphasised, then its surrounding features must be kept low. If a feature is to
be made to look big, then peripheral elements should be kept small. If
light colours (or dark colours) are to be dominant, clear and brilliant,
then their opposite should be placed around them. Buildings and
white walls serve as foils to flowers, trees and rocks; and the smooth
surfaces and clear water of a pool sets off high and craggy hills. *Tai-hu*
rocks, particularly, with all their convolutions and complex surfaces,
need a simple, unadorned background. The white wall is the paper;
the rock, the drawing.

Another example is where the regular shapes of doors, windows

*Figure 3.12: A large building
mass requires a generous
expanse of open space around it
to match its scale and to give it
'breathing room'. The lotus
leaves are removed from the
pond in autumn so that the
surface regains its function as a
mirror of features along its
banks. Zhuo Zheng Yuan,
Suzhou.*

*Figure 3.13: A rock may show
such distinctive form that no
attempt is made to compose it
with other rocks in a grouping
where its special character
might be hidden. Instead,
although its giant size makes it
out of scale with the
surrounding rocks and plants, it
is placed out in the open, alone,
where from all sides it may be
appreciated and admired. It
becomes also a dominant focal
point of emphasis, often where
there is very little else to strike
the eyes of the viewer. Liu
Yuan, Suzhou.*

and roof lines, often dark in colour, contrast with the irregular
outlines of a rocky peak. Similarly, bamboo serves as a good foil to
rocky pinnacles. Where rocky bluffs descend precipitously into a body
of water they appear higher. In each case both dominant and
subordinate elements interact in a balanced treatment, each playing
its own symbiotic role.

Relationships of scale between features are carefully calculated,
especially in small gardens. To make the space seem larger, the buildings should not be too high or too numerous. Otherwise, the primary
space, such as a pond, may become, unintentionally, the secondary
space, overwhelmed by the buildings. In cases where it is necessary to

Figure 3.14: Covered galleries
or breezeways (lang) wind their
zigzag ways, hugging walls or
striking out into the open spaces
of the garden, but never, in
advance, revealing their
ultimate destinations. Small
pockets are created which are
often planted with bamboo or
other light-foliaged plants
whose leaves, in the sunlight,
shine with a luminosity that
sharply contrasts with the
darker walkway and the
shadowy ceiling. Liu Yuan,
Suzhou.

build a multi-storey building within the precincts of a small garden, it
should be placed far back from the pool, and, if possible, with a small,
low, open building placed in front of it at poolside.

Pavilions and kiosks on hills should be small yet finely detailed so
that they appear as independent man-made elements, apart from
their rockery pedestals.

Likewise, trees and shrubs for a small garden should be slow-
growing, finely textured species that are amenable to control of size
through pruning.

Vista and 'Borrowed' Landscapes

The Chinese garden is designed so that the wanderer, as he progresses from point to point, is not only struck by the views of landscape features on either side, at close range or in the middle distance, but is also intrigued by glimpses of vistas ahead of him. The most obvious are the vistas revealed as he moves forward along a path or corridor. Views change after entering through a doorway or making a turn. They may be enframed by a portal or window. For example, through a moon gate one may catch a glimpse of a pond, its lotuses, a particularly evocative rock arrangement, or the inverted reflection of an exquisite pavilion. Besides concern for the front view, lateral views are considered by placing windows and gates along the sides of corridors to enframe exceptionally fine compositions glimpsed as one passes along.

Figure 3.15: In the classical Chinese garden the only extensive open spaces are the ponds and lakes. At suitable points buildings are placed at the water's edge, where, without venturing outside, the inhabitants can have close contact with the water to observe close at hand reflections, ornamental fish, water fowl and aquatic plants, such as waterlilies and lotus. At the same time, views of the sky, unobstructed by trees, are

Of course, the siting of views and vistas is a relative thing. Both observation points and the objects viewed must be interesting and enjoyable in themselves. In effect, they become interdependent, comprising intricate cross vistas. What at one moment is the observation point may become later, as one circumnavigates the garden, the object of another vista.

In addition to the landscape features within the garden, advantage is taken, wherever possible, of evocative landscapes of distant hills and buildings outside the walls. Thus the 'borrowed landscape'

best afforded over expanses of water. The far side of the pond appears further away when seen through the partial screen of rocks and plants. The rocks in the foreground repeat the rocks on the opposite shore, as if they were near and distant mountain ranges. Liu Yuan, Suzhou.

Figure 3.16: The lang *follows the ground's contours, rising and falling with changes in grade. The garden 'traveller' quickly perceives that architecture has adapted itself to nature as it finds it. Zhuo Zheng Yuan, Suzhou.*

becomes a part of the garden's total composition. Conversely, where there is no visible landscape worth 'borrowing', but only unattractive outside features, the garden is planned to screen them out with the placement of hills, trees and architectural visual barriers. But often the sky itself is used as a source of 'borrowed scenery'. By not allowing waterlilies and lotus to obscure the surfaces of ponds and pools, enough uncovered water permits reflection of sky, clouds, the moon, and the garden's own pavilions. This, in a sense, is downward 'borrowed scenery', adding more space and interest to the garden.

Depth and Sequence

The perception of depth in a Chinese garden is enhanced by the long time it takes to penetrate through all its spaces — even though the total area may be relatively small. There is a tortuous system of paths, twists and turns, a roundabout way, no short cuts. At the garden's entrance the line of sight is blocked by walls and hills, thus preventing the visitor from grasping immediately the overall layout.

Besides the perception of depth, the wanderer senses also a sequence of spaces, deeper and more complex as he moves along. Each succeeding space relates in some way to the space that came before. Never completely separated, they are half connected and half

Figure 3.17: Scenes observed at close range should alternate with intriguing long views barely discerned in the distance. The man in the boat is cutting out lotus leaves to clear the water surface. Zhuo Zheng Yuan, Suzhou.

Figure 3.18: An island pavilion reached by bridge or boat provides an observation deck close to the pond's surface. From there the goldfish and carp can almost be touched as they gather for feeding. The reflections of the passing clouds, the surrounding trees, and the moon at night draw the garden wanderer to this sheltered vantage point. Xi Yuan, Suzhou.

Figure 3.19: The cavernous wall of tai-hu *limestone is composed of hundreds of pieces assembled so that the joints are almost invisible, and with their lineaments and contours flowing into each other so as to convey the impression of a monolith. Meanwhile, the scale oscillates between that of a garden rockery, fifteen feet high and the face of a precipitous cliff, looming up hundreds of feet. Only the earthenware planter pot and the pedestal of carved granite stand as reminders that we are in a man-made garden in modest human scale. Liu Yuan, Suzhou.*

Figure 3.20: *Miniature tray landscapes evoke a distant 'world'. For the scale to oscillate one must view them at closer range while eliminating from consciousness all background and supporting elements, including the containers themselves. Shanghai Botanical Garden.*

separated. One finds a suggestion of one feature or material in the succeeding space — in the pavement pattern, for example, or in the repetition of a plant species.

Even where architecture seems to outweigh natural features, such as along corridors and in courtyards, in the small spaces open to the sky are placed modest arrangements of plants (bamboo, banana or maple trees) combined with groupings of *tai-hu* rocks, which can be seen through moon windows and latticed openings. In this way there is an interlarding of natural and man-made features, the former blurring the sharp, incisive outlines of the latter. The perception of greater depth is induced, as well as a clear sequence of spaces and scenic tableaux.

Creating a 'World' with Reverberating Scale

A calming and salubrious atmosphere in the garden is produced by creating illusions of larger space and distant scenery so that one feels an expansion of room, a thrill of release and freedom, as if one had travelled far to view towering mountains. Large gardens, of course, by their very size and location away from the cramped confines of cities and towns, easily display those grand vistas and spaces. But even in small gardens optical tricks, artifices, and the manipulating of space and time cause the viewer to 'discover' distant hills, oceans and islands when actually they are almost within arms' reach.

Such effects are contrived by garden-builders who, themselves, are intimately familiar with every aspect of nature observed in all seasons.

Figure 3.21: Exploiting the
phenomenon of oscillating
scale, it is possible to evoke
vast landscapes of nature with
elements scaled down to fit the
limited space of a walled
courtyard, a room, or even the
miniature confines of a tray,
bowl or urn. Oscillating scale
reverberates in the mind of the
beholder. Thus, at one moment
he may be merely gazing at a
group of ordinary rocks placed
in a naturalistic conformation
along the edge of a pond or
stream. Then, suddenly, a shift
in scale takes place. He is
magically transported far above
the garden's landscape, beyond
its walls, and is gazing down
upon a rocky coastline or at a
distant range of peaks and
precipices.

In this view of a stony shore,
for example, are we not looking
down from a height of at least
five thousand feet upon the
ice-capped coast of Greenland
or Antarctica with its
promontories of glaciers jutting
out into the polar sea? And
those dark objects immobilised
in the frozen pack, are they not
rocky islets or wrecks of boats
trapped in the frozen polar sea
that stretches away to the
distant horizon?

Just as a painter creates a mystical landscape on paper with black ink
and a few strokes of his brush, the garden-builder uncovers the
essences of natural landscape features, and recreates them in a garden
so that, in the viewer's eyes, actual sizes and distances seem to
undergo a transformation. The garden's occult scale takes over. No
longer is it merely a garden, viewed close-up, in conventional proportions. Through an unconscious mental process, the viewer suddenly
sees everything as if he were looking either through the wrong end of
a pair of binoculars, or from high up in the sky, gazing at a distant
shore, a far range of hills, rocky mountain crags or a deep ravine. The
scale oscillates in the spectator's mind. At one moment he is of
human size; but then, alternatively, his perspective changes, and the
scene appears boundless.

Yet another way of instilling a sense of greater space is to introduce
a feature that becomes a metaphor for some aspect of the landscapes
of the real world outside. In this way the beholder is confronted with
an evocative feature that stimulates his imagination. He is seemingly
carried away into a limitless terrain of fantasy. And among all the
landscape metaphors in a Chinese garden the most original and
characteristic are the deeply furrowed and convoluted *tai-hu* rocks.
They may serve as parts of larger rock groupings; or because their
peculiar and expressive lineaments overcome the need to relate in
scale or function to surrounding landscape features, they may simply
stand alone. Often, an especially prized specimen is set upon a base
or platform in an otherwise almost empty courtyard with only a white
plaster wall as its backdrop. It may range in size from a giant formation, far larger than the human body, to a piece as small as a pump-

Figure 3.22: When seen through a semi-transparent screen, in the middle ground of plants and rockery, the far bank of the pond appears more distant. The bright opening below the stone arch increases the perspective. The shrubs and vines growing through the stones and crevices of the nine-foot-high banks make them appear lower. Yi Yuan, Suzhou.

kin. But even the tiniest rock contains a world of its own. It is said in Chinese tradition that a whole mountain is seen in one rock. Such rocks possess, above all other garden materials, that latent power to evoke images, not only of earthly scenes, but even of heaven itself.

For the Chinese, then, rocks have become powerful symbols of the spirit of nature, marvellous for their infinite variety and vividly illustrating the idea of one universal substance forever undergoing cloudlike transformations.

Introducing A Sense of Greater Space and Distance

Overlying the evocative effects produced by rocks and other landscape materials used to make the scale of the garden 'oscillate', the total layout and composition itself reigns as importantly as its details and materials. For centuries the Chinese have applied techniques of composition to fool the eye and to create optical illusions of greater or lesser space. Any and all of the following principles and admonitions may also be readily applied in the West:

Using screens, fences and walls, subdivide one single space into several compartments. One senses, thereby, an increase in the apparent overall space.

Spaces seem larger when seen through semi-transparent or filmy screens and barriers, such as see-through fences or copses of trees. The principle may be tested as follows: with the hand held up eight inches in front of the eyes, and then looking between fingers slightly spread and extending vertically upward, objects beyond seem to recede farther into the background.

Figure 3.23: In allowing the scale to oscillate, the viewer must practise a kind of tunnel vision, eliminating from consciousness all peripheral features which can remind him that he is in a man-made garden. Thus, in these two examples of basaltic cliffs and palisades at the edge of a pond, one must concentrate only on the rocks and their juncture with the water. Soon one imagines seeing those shorelines from a distant viewpoint. The key to creating such an illusion is the placement of the rocks so that they appear as segments of pristine nature. Close-up view: Zhuo Zheng Yuan, Suzhou. Distant view: Yi Yuan, Suzhou.

Set openings and windows in walls and fences so that flashes of parts of other features may be glimpsed beyond. In looking through openings in a succession of walls, gateways or other apertures, the sense of distance increases when the series of openings are seen through alternating patches of light and shade.

Lay out paths so that one's steps are never retraced, or the same view repeated. By winding the walk, even in a small garden, convey

Figure 3.24: The path meanders between rockeries and copses of trees, as if it were a stream winding through a valley enclosed by steep cliffs and flat lowlands. In contrast with the naturalism of the overall layout, the path's mosaic patterns suggest the artistry of man. Liu Yuan, Suzhou.

Figure 3.25: In this corner of a larger courtyard, nature and art are nicely balanced as the rocks and the lacebark pine play against the pebble mosaic pavement, the latticed windows and the tile wall copings. The towering rock assumes a crucial role in the equation, pitting its scale against that of the high wall. The tree on the right is an oleander; on the left a Japanese maple. Wang Shi Yuan, Suzhou.

the idea of a greater extent, and thereby increase both the distance travelled and the time consumed.

Never lay out a walk around the perimeter of a plot of ground, leaving the middle entirely open. The spectator quickly loses interest making the complete circuit with only the open middle continually in view.

Construct paths and spaces of varying widths so that progression

Figure 3.26: First the cheek rocks were set. Then the granite steps were fitted into the gap. Finally, the pebble pavement was laid with provision for planting pockets for vines and mondo grass. Shi Zi Lin, Suzhou.

Figure 3.27: The small garden courtyard offers privacy, not through natural features, but simply by its concealment behind walls. Though it is open to the sky to admit light and air, its only access is from the room which it abuts. The room's occupant may thus position himself outdoors, though in a real sense he remains within the privacy of his rooms. Wang Shi Yuan, Suzhou.

through the garden permits alternatively a sense of constriction and release. The more one feels those changes, the more intense the experience of space and time.

By manipulating relationships of size, textures, colours and tones — changing their relative proportions of weight, quantity or extent — perception of the size of a space can be altered. Thus, placing light-toned, bright objects in the foreground, and dark ones farther away, makes the background recede faster. Planting trees and shrubs with large-leafed foliage in the foreground, and those of finer texture farther away, also makes the background recede faster. Give duller tints to the more distant parts of the composition, and plant there trees of a more subdued colour and of smaller size than those in the foreground. Place larger rocks in the foreground, and smaller ones farther away. Catch the eye with imposing or striking features in the foreground, and place less interesting ones in the background. Apply these principles equally to the composition of pavement patterns.

Vary pavement materials so that one sees a multiplicity of designs and patterns, and feels underfoot alternately smooth and rough textures. The more sensory experiences presented, the larger seems the apparent space.

Make paths narrow down as they approach the horizon, or as seen from the principal point of view. This warping of perspective causes the background to appear farther away.

Suggest the existence of additional spaces, objects or events elsewhere in adjacent areas of the garden by permitting only a part of each to be viewed from any one point at any given moment.

Do not reveal completely from one point the shoreline of a pond or other body of water. In that way one cannot be sure of its full extent. Promontories, coves and islands conceal a pond's true boundaries.

Construct paths, galleries, tunnels in hills, subterranean passages and changes in gradients that slow down the visitor, causing him to pause, catch his breath, and thus protract his time in the garden.

Lay out a garden so that one hears sounds from moving water, wind chimes, bells, human voices, birds in cages, wind hissing in pine trees, and rustling of leaves in bamboo groves. They slow down the visitor as he pauses to listen, and add ingredients to the total of his sensory experience.

Deep thickets and boldly winding paths dispel the idea of a garden boundary. With deftly calculated grading and planting, the real boundaries of a garden (its outer wall) are concealed so that appropriate and pleasing outside landscape features appear as natural extensions — so-called 'borrowed' scenery. Further, take advantage of outside features by repeating them in scaled-down form within the garden so that they seem to blend together. For example, build up a hillock which appears as the foothill of higher elevations beyond the wall. Or, plant trees of the same species inside the garden that appear over the garden wall on the outside. In that way they become one continuous forest.

Change the ratios of scale of elements of the garden: scaled-down objects in a given space make that space seem larger, and vice versa.

As in atmospheric landscape paintings, where space is occupied by the suggestion of clouds and mist to give the impression of looking into the depths of a distant landscape, so too, in a garden, the same illusion may be produced by using plants whose flowers or seed heads are hazy, mist-like and finely textured. For example, such an effect is produced by planting copses of smoketrees (*Cotinus coggygria*) in a series of receding planes.

Erect tablets with ancient inscriptions, verses and moral precepts. Such philosophical statements on tablets and plaques acquire a strange force in themselves, and, at the same time, can enhance the predominant mood of the place. Poetry in gardens stimulates the larger world of the mind. The more varieties of experience in a garden — both sensory and intellectual — the larger seems the garden.

Studied disorderliness imparts the feeling of the infinite, and makes one imagine the garden to be larger than it is.

The nub of the principles cited here were expressed by the eighteenth-century writer, Shen Fu, in his book *Fusheng Liuqi* (*Six Chapters of a Floating Life*):

Show the large in the small and the small in the large; provide for the real in the unreal, and for the unreal in the real.

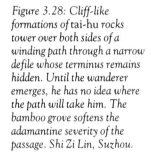

Figure 3.28: Cliff-like formations of tai-hu rocks tower over both sides of a winding path through a narrow defile whose terminus remains hidden. Until the wanderer emerges, he has no idea where the path will take him. The bamboo grove softens the adamantine severity of the passage. Shi Zi Lin, Suzhou.

As to the planning of garden pavilions and towers, of winding corridors and kiosks, and in the designing of rockery, or the training of flowering trees, one should try to show the small in the large and the large in the small ... One reveals and conceals alternately, making it sometimes apparent and sometimes hidden. This is not just 'rhythmic irregularity', nor does it depend on having a wide space and great expenditure of labour and material. Pile up a mound with earth dug from the ground, and arrange upon it groupings of rocks and plants. Use live plum branches for your fence, and plant creepers over the walls. Thus, there will be a hill in a place which is without hills. In the large open spaces plant bamboos that grow quickly, and train plum trees with thick branches to mask parts of them. This is to show the small in the large.

When the courtyard is small, the wall should be a combination of convex and concave shapes, decorated with green, covered with ivy, and inlaid with big slabs of stone with inscriptions on them. Thus, when you open the window, you seem to face a rocky hillside, alive with rugged beauty. This is to show the large in the small.

Contrive so that an apparently blind alley leads suddenly into an

Figure 3.29: Even a narrow skylit niche, surrounded on three sides by off-white stucco walls, ten feet high, contains the elements of nature that enliven an otherwise drab space: bamboo that captures the fleeting sunlight, a shaft of natural limestone rock evocative of mountain peaks, and broadleaf deciduous shrubs. Such confined settings serve as symbolic dioramas, viewed daily by the garden's users as they pass to and fro along covered passageways and galleries, such as this one, that link halls, pavilions and courtyards. Liu Yuan, Suzhou.

open space, and the kitchen leads through a back door into an unexpected courtyard. This is to provide for the real in the unreal. Let a door lead into a blind courtyard and conceal the view by placing a few canes of bamboo and a few rocks. Thus, suggest something which is not there. Place low balustrades along the top of a wall so as to suggest a roof garden which does not exist. This is to provide for the unreal in the real.

Figure 3.30: The raised planting beds, retained by massive rockery, provide spaces for a variety of both woody and herbaceous trees, shrubs and flowers, which bloom intermittently from spring through autumn. Viewed from the house, the combination of plantings and stonework appear as a fragment of uncultivated nature introduced into the living space. Mixing broadleaf and needle evergreen with deciduous species assures maintenance of the plantings' structure even in winter. Liu Yuan, Suzhou.

Finding Privacy

Traditionally, personal privacy was rare in China, where often three generations of a family lived together inside a walled compound. If privacy was not possible to find within the close quarters of domestic housing, individual members of more affluent families often could attain some measure of isolation, away from relatives and servants, in the recesses of the garden, pavilions and small courtyards that were spotted throughout the open spaces separating the houses of the various family branches.

Outdoor spaces were compartmented by garden walls, eight to ten feet high, and by the strategic placement of hills, rockery masses, earth mounds, tree and shrub copses and bamboo groves. Paths and covered passageways twisted and meandered around and through the topography and plantings. Paths also led up and down hills and through rock grottoes, and often dead-ended in cavernous underground chambers. In this almost maze-like landscape of hills and dales there were only short sight lines. It was possible, therefore, to find privacy either in remote, secluded courtyards, woody glens, or in the bowels of the rockeries.

The garden became a place of refuge, away from the restraints of rigidly enforced etiquette, and possible family censure and criticism. In the garden one found a sense of relief and freedom.

Figure 3.31: A quiet retreat in a sunny courtyard of deciduous trees and stone benches away from the rest of the garden's activity. The chequerboard mosaic pavement consists of light-hued pebbles and darker stone shards. The latticed windows are inspired by both geometry, flowers and fruits. Cang Lang Ting, Suzhou.

Figure 3.32: The sunny courtyard inspires a cheerful mood, introduced by the plantings and the view of the low tiled roof with the trees on the other side. Privacy resides here, but also a liveliness generated by art: the lines of the neighbouring tiled roof, lattices and the pebble mosaic in the stylised plum blossom motif. Zhuo Zheng Yuan, Suzhou.

Stimulating Fantasy

Evidence of the attraction to fantasy appears on all levels of Chinese life, from religious rites to mundane daily occupations. Natural and man-made environments abound with signs and symbols, derived from myth and legend, that appeal to the Chinese appetite for allegory, for wanting to penetrate beyond the obvious by reaching below the surface of objects and events. In family relationships, business and government, as well as in the arts, the well-marked way is avoided in favour of ambiguity. In gardens the preference for allusion and imagery is satisfied by both the choice of specific materials and in their arrangement and configurations. The fantasies thus evoked follow familiar and worn paths into the human psyche.

There is, for example, escapism: the yearning to flee from one's present situation. It may be appeased by placing architecture hedged in among sharp crags or sheltered in the recesses of a valley surrounded by hills. The world then seems far away, even if it is only over the garden wall. Or, the feeling of being lost in a wilderness may be elicited by creating a garden setting which is a scaled-down abstraction, symbolic of a famous wild landscape.

Memories are evoked by placing in a garden flowering plants with haunting fragrances, or by objects in the garden having associations with people and events from the past.

There can be an appeal to human sensuality through placement in the garden of objects with earthy associations, on both conscious and unconscious levels (rocks, for example, with genital forms, in several Suzhou gardens).

Rockery may also stimulate fantasy with humour and amusement. Thus, the playful stone 'lions' in a courtyard of 'Shi Zi Lin' (Stone Lion Grove) create a light-hearted mood.

Myths, poetry, recollections of historical happenings, and symbolic associations are evoked in the selection of plants and architectural details and motifs. Tablets, for example, with poetic inscriptions, over a portal set the mood of a courtyard by initiating a train of thought or day-dreaming in the mind of the viewer. There is evocative symbolism, too, in the biomorphic and geometrical motifs of window lattices, and the decorative finials and ornamentation of gargoyles, mythical deities, dragons and lions on roof ridges and along wall copings.

Symbolism in plants embraces a variety of species. Apple denotes peace; apricot, cherry, magnolia, jasmine, orchid and azalea stand for the fair sex and feminine beauty; bamboo, pine, plum and pear are signs of longevity; orange and Buddha's hand are for wealth and prosperity; pomegranate betokens posterity and many progeny, while persimmon means joy; peony suggests good fortune and love; chrysanthemum, joviality; lotus is the sign of fruitfulness, Buddhism and Taoism; willow stands for suppleness and meekness, while oak is for masculine strength.

Figure 3.33: The huge scale of these tai-hu limestone monoliths requires their placement in wide open spaces which they dominate and where they may be appreciated from a distance. Standing like sentinels, some with biomorphic form, others appearing as mountain peaks, they introduce into the essentially bland landscape of trees and shrubs a sense of mystery and wonder at nature's strange shapes. And, while taken in bulk, they can be viewed as elements of strength, the delicate tracery and wispiness of their separate parts suggests a lightness and buoyancy ready to float off at any moment. This is especially true when they are seen through early morning mists. They are examples of the often encountered oscillating duality which never fails to intrigue the Chinese garden amateur. Zhuo Zheng Yuan, Suzhou.

Figure 3.34: Wherever possible, no matter how restricted the space, every opportunity is taken to present a composition of rocks and plants that will symbolise a poet's or painter's conception of a distant mountain landscape. Here, the rock peaks seem to thrust through clouds of sunlit, luminous bamboo foliage. The bright foreground is surrounded by a covered gallery whose shadowy walls are pierced, in turn, by a doorway leading to another bright area beyond. Thus there occurs the succession of light and dark spaces encountered typically in Chinese gardens. Wang Shi Yuan, Suzhou.

Figure 3.35: Tai-hu limestone rocks composed in animal forms are the most striking features of the courtyard. The stone 'lions' cavort among the rocky peaks and ridges. Even the ceramic trash receptacle's top in the form of a frog seems to participate in the 'games' of these playful 'creatures'. It is a clear example of the evocation of imagination and fantasy through rock arrangement. Shi Zi Lin, Suzhou.

Figure 3.36: The rock, like a great bear, rears up as if it were guarding the wall, which seems puny in comparison. The trees are large enough to reduce the huge stone's imposing scale. Yi Yuan, Suzhou.

Figure 3.37: The dragon's antennae are repeated in the delicate tracery of the vine in the upper right-hand corner. Yu Yuan, Shanghai.

Figure 3.38: Although the rockery is set a short distance from structures, its arrangement conveys the feeling of a remote mountain fastness far from civilisation. It is composed of limestone tai-hu rocks so skilfully joined that the effect is of a monolithic mass of crags and peaks in fantastic forms and configurations suggesting a community of animals. Liu Yuan, Suzhou.

Banishing Monotony: Producing Mystery and Surprise

The Chinese classical garden makes a conscious attempt to play upon the emotions, sensory perceptions, and, even at times, to induce fear and to test one's capacity to accept frustration. The garden wanderer, for instance, wishing to go from point A to point B, ponders how to get there. Does the path he is following lead to his intended destination, or to a dead-end? Mystification, making senses swim, is a built-in theme. It's the old Chinese puzzle of box inside box inside box, seemingly *ad infinitum*.

What may be apparent from a distance on the other side of a wall aperture may, upon passing through, turn out, when seen at close range, to be an object or scene quite different from what one had expected.

Mystery is created by sounds from an unseen and undefined source, heard over a wall, fence, or through a thick copse of trees, or emerging from within a nearby pavilion, gallery or adjacent covered passageway. The ear may be struck by voices and the eye tantalised with a confused sight of figures, seen dimly through the stems and foliage of trees.

Wall elevations reflect the garden's topography. They rise and fall

Figure 3.39: A covered gallery with many openings in its walls, and leading to more than two destinations, imparts a mood of anticipation, uncertainty and mystery. The passer-by is offered a number of choices as to which path to follow and which door to enter. The bright openings of the windows and the archway over water present tantalising prospects of the scenes that lie beyond. The tree in foreground is a crape myrtle. Zhuo Zheng Yuan, Suzhou.

Figure 3.40: A grotto of basaltic 'yellow' rock. Grottoes stir a sense of adventure and mystery, providing hiding places for children of all ages, and a cool, dark retreat in summer from the heat and glare of the sun. Thus the shifting feeling of coolness and warmth may be experienced along with the contrasts of light and dark. This grotto is constructed of basaltic 'yellow' rock, hard metamorphosed igneous material. The centre of gravity of each rock is firmly supported by underlying or surrounding rocks, so that even if the mortar in the joints should become dislodged, the rocks will not move. Wang Shi Yuan, Suzhou.

with the land. But often plantings or rockery will be used to hide the precise point where the top of a wall rises or falls, particularly in the case of an abrupt change of grade. The eye is fooled as to the location of that change.

A sure cause for surprise and banishment of monotony is the 'light-box effect'. Objects such as trees, planter tubs, *bonsai*, artifacts and rocks, seen through doorways and wall openings, appear to assume different forms that shift with changes in the intensity and direction of natural light falling upon them. Thus, back, frontal or flank lighting produce different visual effects in texture, colour and shape to attract interest from dawn to dusk.

Marking Time

In China it is believed that frequent reminders from nature of the passage of time, presented in all its aspects, help one experience the fullness of life. And from the earliest times it was understood that if one could not get away to make direct contact with undiluted nature in some remote mountain fastness, then a garden was an acceptable path for observing time's flight. Garden paths were laid out and kiosks and verandas located so that the wanderer, at every turn, would encounter sights and sounds to impress upon his consciousness the passing of time.

In effect, time assumed five aspects — momentary, diurnal, seasonal, generational, and eternal — all of which, at different points and moments, would manifest themselves to the man of taste and sensibility.

Passage of momentary time was demonstrated, for example, by the interval it took for a leaf, floating downstream, to disappear under a bridge and then to reappear on the opposite side, by the regular rasping buzz of a cicada in summer, or the accumulation of falling snowflakes on a rock or pine boughs.

Evidence of diurnal time's movement was shown, as the day wore on, in the shifting patterns of shadows of branches and foliage cast on a garden wall, by the opening of morning-glories and day-lilies in the morning and their closing at night, the passage through the night sky from dusk to dawn of the moon and planets, or the gradual melting of snow and ice as they are struck by the transit of the sun's rays.

The annual progress of the seasons denotes longer intervals of time which appeal to the human desire for change and hope in the future. Thus, spring brings renewal, warmth and blooming; summer, growth and maturing; autumn, cessation of growth, harvest, leaves turning and dropping; and finally, winter, cold slowing the pace of nature, and repose.

Indications of generational time may be seen in the growth of a tree in one's own lifetime from memories of childhood to old age, the weathering and ageing of the surfaces of buildings and artifacts as seen in the gradual formation over the years of patina on bronze and copper, and the growth of lichens on rocks.

Finally, the inertial pace of time in its eternal aspect is shown in the seemingly unchanging forms of a garden's adamantine granites and basalts — resistant rock formations formed in the earth's basic mantle during eons of prehistoric time.

Touching Nature with a Roof Overhead

In Chinese thought there is the recurring image of man in intimate contact with nature. Paintings depict the hermit on a mountainside, facing a ribbon of waterfall, often with a rude hut in the background, surrounded by misty crags and pines, and confronting the emptiness of space. Poetry describes reactions to all these phenomena.

Figure 3.41: From the veranda and gallery the garden-viewer is brought face to face with the lush trees and shrubs whose foliage and blossoms appear and fade with the changing seasons. The plantings wrap the building so tightly that it is possible simply to reach out, touch and examine them at close range, as if one's eyes were microscopes. The arrival of spring is announced by the pale green leaves on the bamboo and Japanese maple, and the yellow flowers of the loquat tree. June brings the white fragrant jasmine growing through the rocks of the pond embankment, and the succulent fruit of the loquat. The arrival of autumn is marked by the Japanese maple's leaves as they turn from green to scarlet. Yi Yuan, Suzhou.

Similarly, in gardens, the same intimacy is sought. There, however, it must be worked in with the mundane requirements of a functioning family compound where easy communication between its sectors must be facilitated in all seasons and under all weather conditions. Hence, the resort to roofed galleries and *lang* (covered passageways) that thread their way through gardens, and to the strategic siting of pavilions.

Passing from place to place, the resident, as well as the visitor, may observe from such shelters, at close range, and often within touching distance, the natural landscape of plantings, rockery and water features. From the security of a roof overhead may be witnessed the effects upon the garden's features of weather in all its forms as it occurs. Without venturing too far from the familiarity and comfort of architecture, the garden wanderer can become an attentive daily spectator of nature's changing moods.

Figure 3.42: Fishing from one's house is touching nature with a roof overhead. Painting, part of a handscroll: 'The Garden For Self-enjoyment' by Qiu Ying (ca. 1522-1560). Courtesy of The Cleveland Museum of Art, Purchase, John. L. Severance Fund.

Blending Nature with Art

The Chinese penchant for architectural elaboration, intricate detailing, and even the painting of wood surfaces makes transitions from architecture to nature seem, at first glance, incongruous and abrupt. Closer observation and analysis, however, reveals a sensitive juxtaposing and fusion of man-made with naturalistic elements.

It may be simply the harmony of tones in a cut-stone balustrade with similar shades in the surrounding rockery. At times, the same stone material may be fashioned into architectural shapes of posts and beams, or used as pebbles in a mosaic pavement. A natural rock with a flat surface may serve as a step leading from a veranda on to an expanse of pavement. And pavilions and galleries, artfully sited among hills and rockeries, seem to fit naturally into the landscape despite their obvious architectural lines. The harmony is facilitated by the delicacy of columns and beams, and the curving roof lines. Walls

Figure 3.43: First the rocks were placed to retain a hill and to convey the impression of a steep escarpment. Then the wall was built around the rocks as if it were accommodating pre-existing palisades. The undulating coping of the wall could represent ocean waves breaking on a rocky shore. Zhuo Zheng Yuan, Suzhou.

follow the rising and falling contours of the earth, almost as if they had grown out of it. The edges of pavements next to rockery are generally irregular, as they follow the ins and outs of the abutting rock profiles.

Nature is introduced into the recesses of buildings in the many small interior courtyards which provide light and ventilation for back rooms, and, at the same time, give space for plantings and rock arrangements.

Another means of bringing nature and art together is the placement of structures partly over water along shorelines to convey the feeling of an architecture intimately joined with the natural element of water.

Finally, other creatures of nature, such as fish in ponds and birds in cages, are brought into the garden, and biomorphic symbols in the form of flowers, fruits and vegetables, become the patterns for door frames, windows and latticework.

Figure 3.44: The marriage of nature and art is dramatically expressed by the intimate conjunction of the rocky irregularity of the shoreline with its ancient gnarled tree, and the regular lines of the building with its exquisite window latticework. The cochlea spiral in the round window, though a symmetrical work of art, suggests nature in the pure form of a snailshell, or the helical flare of the sun. Cang Lang Ting, Suzhou.

Figure 3.45: The small, intimate courtyard offers a sunny private space easily accessible from the contiguous living quarters. In rainy weather the veranda gives shelter. The nearby plum trees blossom in early spring. The undulating wall evokes images of distant hills and mountain ranges. The rock step set into the pavement at the edge of the veranda serves an architectural function with a purely natural form, and thereby introduces the first physical contact with nature as one leaves the house. Zhuo Zheng Yuan, Suzhou.

Figure 3.46: The sharp rhythmic patterns of the leaves are echoed in the roof tiles' projections. Liu Yuan, Suzhou.

Plate 1.
Both seclusion and a sense of
illimitable space is achieved for
the pavilion and its paved
courtyard by arranging the
rocks and plantings in depth.
The dark undulating wall seems
to recede into the shadows
created by the tall trees and
evergreen shrubbery. Salvia
relieves the pervasive
monochrome of the masonry
and foliage. Zhuo Zheng Yuan,
Suzhou.

Plates 2 and 3. The perfect roundness of a gateway or window softens the straight architectural lines of its immediate space. The contrast is accentuated when the near side is in shadow or darkness which the viewer's eyes must penetrate before fastening onto the bright scene on the other side. Plate 2: Zhuo Zheng Yuan, Suzhou. Plate 3: Yi Yuan, Suzhou.

Plate 4. The ting pavilion is built on a ridge, yet is pulled back from the summit which is reserved for rockery and planting, rather than a man-made structure. Zhuo Zheng Yuan, Suzhou.

Plate 5: From the ting pavilion, situated on the hill, may be glimpsed overall views of the garden. Yet, as seen from afar, it remains secluded behind a screen of trees and shrubs, and the winding course of the rock steps that lead up to it. Zhuo Zheng Yuan, Suzhou.

Plate 6. The precipitous rocks along the high banks of the pond's inlet suggest the cliffs of the Yangtze River gorges. The rocks' parallel planes, both vertical and horizontal, convey a sense of permanent repose and final settlement, as is found frequently in nature after eons of metamorphosis. This evocation of grand landscapes outside the garden comes to the garden 'traveller' while he is under the protection of the covered walkways — lang. Zhuo Zheng Yuan, Suzhou.

Plate 7. The covered walkways
(lang) provide, during
inclement weather, dry
connections between pavilions.
It is architecture penetrating
and encompassing the natural
elements of the garden in ways
far more affecting than can be
achieved by halls and pavilions.
In hot weather the lang offers
shady pathways to the garden's
farthest reaches. Liu Yuan,
Suzhou.

Plate 8. The rock's upper section is massive in contrast to its thin connection to the ground. Yet it appears well balanced and, in fact, weightless, defying gravity. The sinuous lines of the Japanese maple's branches and the delicacy of its leaves add the right polarity, opposing the rock's mass. Wang Shi Yuan, Suzhou.

Plate 9. Trees, shrubbery and salvia flowers form the Yang element of dynamic growth to counterbalance the Yin of the taihu rocks' earthly base. Cang Lang Ting, Suzhou.

Plate 10. Undulating shapes of the taihu rocks seem to come alive, swarming over the landscape as if they were a colony of grimacing animals from another world. The path, built into the rockery, leads the garden visitor through the rugged labyrinth to reach all parts of the stony 'swarm'. Shi Zi Lin, Suzhou.

Plate 11. With wide expanses of still water, the reflections of the sky, as much as the buildings and trees, become a vital element of the garden's design. Li Yuan, Wuxi.

Plate 12. By placing the rockery
along the shore so that it
touches the architecture, the
evocation of nature's wild
landscapes is made more vivid.
And, as if to counterbalance the
rampant natural forms of the
rockery, the mind and spirit of
man is represented by the stone
finial of a Buddhist stupa
emerging from the water's
surface. Zhuo Zheng Yuan,
Suzhou.

Plate 13. Water, rockery, architecture and plants closely intermesh in a small garden where space is limited. Juxtaposition of these four elements occur one after the other without the relieving intervention of purely natural landscapes to offset their concentration. Wang Shi Yuan, Suzhou.

Plate 14. Irregular rocky shorelines of promontories, bays and inlets add to the perception of infinite space. Here, taihu limestone is pieced together to form high craggy bluffs and low jagged fringes at water level. As in nature, rockery is interrupted by plants and sandy, marshy edges providing relief from over-dependence on rocks. Li Yuan, Wuxi.

Plate 15. Mature, tall trees not only impart a feeling of age to the garden, but also cause the wall and buildings to appear reduced in height, and the banks of the pond to seem more low-lying. Cang Lang Ting, Suzhou.

Plate 16. The high and low arrangement of basaltic rocks in their concave and convex patterns evoke images of landscapes of uplifted cliffs, water caves and quiet coves. Their reflections heighten the effect. Diao Yutai, Beijing.

Plate 17. Courtyards of
Chinese houses provide privacy
and serve as escape valves,
offering convenient temporary
relief from the pressures of
domestic life. There one can sit
under a tree and meditate, or
stroll by constructed rockeries,
fantasizing travel through the
passes of far off mountains.
Cang Lang Ting, Suzhou.

Plate 18. The outsize scale of the bronze urns and figures, and the absence of intimate plantings are indications of the awesome grandeur pervading the palaces and gardens of the former imperial court of China. Guggong, Beijing.

Plate 19. Mosaic pavement. Yi Yuan, Suzhou.

Plate 20. Both Chinese and Japanese gardens alternate dark and light, and constriction and release to enhance the viewer's sense of greater space and to offer a more complex aesthetic experience. Japanese garden, Pocantico Hills, New York.

Figure 3.47: A perfect balance exists in this secluded courtyard between features of pure architecture — white walls, the lattice geometry of the windows, and elegant roof lines — and the elements of pure nature — rocks and plants. The random irregular stone pavement serves as a transitional element: flat rocks broken into natural forms, yet used in a completely architectural context. The feeling is one of a complete draw between nature and art. The trees are Japanese maples; the shrubs, hydrangeas, aucuba and mondo grass. Wang Shi Yuan, Suzhou.

Figure 3.48: A wall develops a more unobtrusive character when it appears to follow the ground's natural contours, or even if it follows man-made hills and swales. In either case, the wall seems to cling to the ground as though it were a natural fringe, or a sinuous creature such as a giant serpent or worm inexorably inching its way over the landscape. The wall becomes an organic piece of architecture, far different from stepped walls and panels. Beihai Park, Beijing.

Allocating Space for Family and Friends

Since so much of the activity and attention of the Chinese extended family was concentrated upon their mutual interest — the promotion and enhancement of their lives and fortunes — it became necessary to provide convenient and suitable spaces (both indoors and outdoors) where family members and retainers could assemble and congregate. Etiquette and custom, moreover, required segregation and allotment of space for varying degrees of formality and class levels. In this way privacy was maintained while social position and forms were observed.

In addition, since the garden was not only the physical matrix binding together the various family sectors, but also the vehicle for bringing the family closer to nature, there had to be provided vantage points, in a sense, observation platforms, of adequate size and acceptable design, from which nature might be appreciated. Fulfilment of those needs resulted in courtyards and open spaces for moon viewing, poetry writing contests, and other aesthetic endeavours.

Figure 3.49: Painting, part of a handscroll: 'The Literary Gathering at a Yangzhou Garden' by Fang Shi Xu (1692-1751). Courtesy of The Cleveland Museum of Art, Purchase, The Severance and Greta Millikin Purchase Fund.

Appealing with Abstract Patterns and Forms

Completely isolated from their peculiar native cultural context, some aspects and features of a Chinese classical garden may still be enjoyed purely for the satisfaction and pleasure they provide as abstract designs. Consciously and unconsciously, whether they are simple or complex, they are enjoyed as works of art. They possess the characteristic qualities of good composition: balance, unity, contrast, rhythm. Or, their forms are symbols of familiar objects cherished by the garden artist and by those who will view the garden. They may be appreciated simply for their intrinsic beauty and outward symbolism, such as doorways in the conventionalised four-lobed figure of a plum blossom, a window shaped like a fan, or the cracked ice pattern in a pebble mosaic pavement. In addition, some designs are metaphors with hidden meanings appealing on a deeper level to those 'in the know'.

But on whatever level a particular feature is enjoyed, the garden viewer must practice concentration. Just as a photographer crops out distracting, irrelevant parts of a picture to create his own composition, so must the garden wanderer focus on his selected features of interest while ignoring those in the foreground, background or periphery which spoil or detract from his view of the central point of interest.

Notes

[1] Abode of the Immortals, godlike sages, believed by ancient Chinese to live on islands off the coast of Shantung Province.

Figure 3.50: The symmetry of this entry forecourt of the Lion Grove Garden expresses a formality not often found in a Chinese garden. There is a central axis paved in granite slabs running through the middle. The balanced composition of two ginkgo trees, and two sago palms in tubs accentuates the bilateral arrangement. The light on the back wall, rather than suggesting confinement, causes the wall to look like fog or mist — as if one could walk right through it into white clouds. Shi Zi Lin, Suzhou.

Figure 3.51: Simply paved courtyards, such as this, were reserved for formal functions as well as for gatherings of family and friends. Its uncomplicated bilateral symmetry implies seriousness, sobriety and a direct approach, rare in Chinese gardens. In the days when the garden was the private domain of one extended family its patriarch would sit on a throne-like chair or couch placed in the doorway (at the rear of the picture), and would grant audiences there, conduct family business, or play host to family members and business associates invited to watch entertainments performed by actors, dancers and musicians. Cang Lang Ting, Suzhou.

Figure 3.52: Ceramic grillework: Zhuo Zheng Yuan, Suzhou.

Figure 3.53: Wall coping: tile. Nanjing.

Figure 3.54: Window grillework: glazed ceramic. Wall and roof coping: tile. Yu Yuan, Shanghai.

Chapter 4
Garden Features and Materials:
Design and Construction Techniques

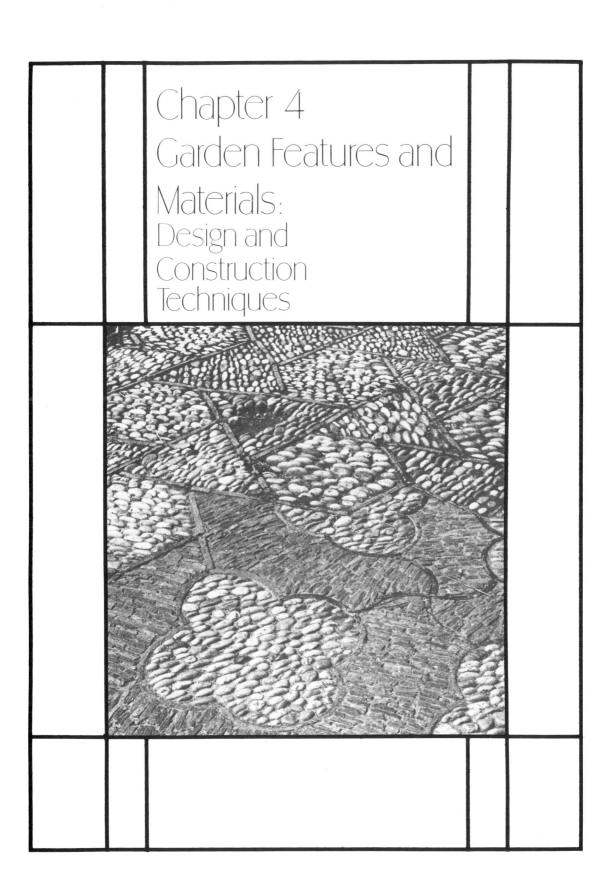

Water

The mirror of the pond reflects the shadows;
here is opened an entrance to the mermaid's
palace . . . The moon shines through the
willow trees by the pond when it washes its
soul in the clear water.
'Yuan Ye'

A garden lake is 'like an aperture in the world,
through which you see another
world, another sun and other skies.'
Sir William Chambers

Impressed by the irresistible power of water in moulding the natural landscape, garden-builders from early times made water a key element, as well, in the composition of their classical hill and water landscapes. Water was readily available in the *Jiangnan* garden cities of Suzhou, Wuxi, Yangzhou and Hangzhou, all situated either by lakes, rivers or canals in the Yangtze Valley — a plain with a high water table. Under those conditions it was easy even for a commoner to excavate a pond and keep it filled with water.

The garden pool's bright surface formed a clear, unobstructed liquid sheet that sharply contrasted with the landscape's intricate elements, illustrating in one more way the close correlation of opposites: sparse and dense, open and closed, light and dark. The pool became a mirror, reflecting the trees, rocks and architecture around its perimeter, as well as the sky above, clouds and the moon. It provided, too, the watery medium for *koi*, the large golden, pink and white carp-like fish swimming in Chinese garden pools and ponds. And aside from aesthetics, the utilitarian value of a body of water in a garden was never minimised. A pool helped regulate the humidity, purify the air, and served as a handy reservoir of water in case of fire.

Pond Design

In small gardens one consolidated body of water lends a feeling of openness and clarity. Where a hilly island or zigzag bridge divides the body of water into two or more irregularly shaped ponds, the space seems endless because it is difficult to tell where it ends. Such division is preferable in larger gardens. But the ponds should not be equal in size. There should be a primary and a subordinate water feature, and a clear distinction made between the two. But even in one pond, bends and irregularities in the shoreline can make it seem larger and the water source far away.

A boundary between primary and secondary pools may be either a peninsula or an island surrounded by a narrow neck of water. Where the rockery hill is the main scenic feature, the ribbon-like pool may weave in and out around its base forming shallow coves and inlets. It makes the hill seem higher and steeper.

In a small garden where the pool is long, narrow and twisting, a bridge can serve to divide the water into primary and secondary sections.

Bridges, usually of stone beams, are placed over the narrow necks of water. Often they zigzag over eight turns. The larger the body of water, the higher the bridge, and the higher the bridge, the more it appears to unify the space above it with the land on both ends of the bridge. At the same time the bridge's inverted reflection appears more prominent on the water surface. Conversely, over small bodies of water bridges are nestled close to the surface. Then, in contrast, nearby cliffs lining the shore appear loftier.

Bridge railings are generally rectangular flat stone slabs fixed along both sides of the bridge, and set low. Occasionally, irregular *tai-hu*

Figure 4.1: The bridge serves not only as a functional link across the pond, but also as a viewing platform when the lotuses are in bloom in summer. The zigzag shape forces one to slow down and to view the scene from changing angles as one advances across. The bridge is constructed of granite slabs. Zhuo Zheng Yuan, Suzhou.

rocks are used as low railing along the edges of a bridge. Although simple wooden spans are rare, large and intricately designed covered wooden bridges are commonly found in a number of Suzhou gardens.

Where a stream or gully is traversed by a path, stepping-stones, at least eighteen inches in diameter, may be used in place of a bridge.

Banks and Shorelines

As in nature, the banks of garden ponds and pools surrounded by flat terrain have low, gentle slopes to the water, while garden pools surrounded by 'hills' and 'mountains', have precipitous and high, rocky banks. Often there are rocks jutting out over the water. But rarely does one see a bank, composed only of soil, without the reinforcement at the waterline of even a narrow protective edging of small rocks and stones. It would soon be eroded by water action. Earth banks are successful only where there is enough space to permit very gradual slopes to the water's edge. Even so, it is necessary to plant some species of natural groundcover, such as grasses or reeds, whose roots will hold the soil in place. An alternative groundcover is a layer of river stone pebbles, over which creep vines and other spreading groundcovers.

Figure 4.2: The irregular composition of basaltic rocks of the shoreline, in the foreground, is repeated in the natural arrangement of rocks of similar material retaining the high planting bed on the left. By contrast, however, the paved raised terrace in front of the building, upper left, is defined at the water's edge by the straight architectural line of cut granite slabs. The geometry of the pavement accommodates itself to the natural coves and promontories of the rocks. Zhuo Zheng Yuan, Suzhou.

Figure 4.3: Whenever it rains, water wetting rocks, pavements and the granite bridge ties these three features together, and links them, in turn, to the pond. The poles buttress trees with extreme slants. Wang Shi Yuan, Suzhou.

Banks retained by natural rocks are composed of either basaltic 'yellow rock' or by limestone lake rocks. Rarely are they mixed within one composition or as part of the same natural feature. But with either material the rightness of their composition — their appearance of belonging, of naturalness — is determined by how well each rock relates to its adjoining neighbour. Attention must be paid to matching their veins and shapes so that, as a whole, they appear to belong to each other. The lines of one rock must appear to continue in the rock placed next to it. Shoreline rocks must always look as if nature, not man, had placed them. Both large and small rocks are used, some projecting higher than others. Concave curves, alternating with convex, are uneven and undulating. Gaps in the rockery are randomly spaced to provide soil pockets for plantings. Some rocks jut out over the water to form water caves that look like gaping dark mouths conveying the sense of vaster expanses far beyond the

immediately visible shoreline. Some of the higher rocks are placed not only to give undulation to the embankment, but also to provide flat sites for seating.

In no case, however, does the stone bank appear so stiff or high as to make the water look as if it were contained in a deep well surrounded by a parapet. Often, for the convenience of actual closer contact with the water, natural rocks are arranged as steps descending to the water's edge. And, at the water's edge, large, flat rocks are set, often out into the water, mostly submerged but with their top surfaces exposed several inches above the water line to form a small, natural terrace that contrasts with the vertical lines of the rocky precipice at its back.

Where pavilions and covered galleries are placed along the banks of ponds, their terraces and foundations are held by retaining walls of cut, dressed stone slabs laid up in waterside revetments. They introduce into the naturalistic shoreline of rocks and plantings a strong sense of architecture and human activity.

A waterside revetment wall of dressed stone slabs stands out as a

Figure 4.4: Natural stone steps deftly built into the high rockery shoreline provide the garden 'traveller' with the means to gain intimate contact with the water. Plantings of jasmine and bamboo among the rocks soften the hard surfaces and tie the water's edge to the surrounding landscaping. Zhuo Zheng Yuan, Suzhou.

strong architectural feature contraposed against the mass of natural elements of rocks and plants. It is therefore essential, in order not to appear outlandish, that it be well constructed of slabs that relate in colour and texture to the natural rocks. The courses should be horizontal and roughly parallel to the water surface and to the horizontal lines of nearby buildings. The slabs should be rectangular, though at times it may be appropriate to mix in a few irregular natural rocks that tie in and relate to nearby natural rockery.

Aside from the still water of ponds and lakes, Chinese classical gardens also contain water in motion: cascades, falls and streams, but never fountains. A brook cascading down a hillside may be fed by water led inside from higher elevations outside the garden. And in other instances, they are designed to flow only during rain storms, when run-off water from roofs is piped to flow over the cascades or into the streams. Their rock work is so well done, moreover, that even during fair weather, when dry, they look natural. The streams are laid out in sinuous courses that wind through rocks and plantings to convey the feeling of origination at a distant source.

Figure 4.5: The covered walkway smoothly insinuates its course past the rocks of the shoreline, which had been set earlier. No attempt is made to hold the pavement and stone balustrade level. They rise and fall with the natural contours of the embankment. Cang Lang Ting, Suzhou.

Mountains, Hills and Rockery

From the earliest years of the Western Han Dynasty rockery appeared as a distinguishing feature in the hills of Chinese gardens. Later, by Tang and Sung times, garden rockery techniques reached a high level of artistry, especially influenced by the work of landscape painters. To render faithfully their subjective interpretations of natural rock formations, both painters and garden craftsmen went to the wild to study the characteristics and configurations of rocks on mountains and cliffs, in caves and along shorelines.

During the latter dynasties of Ming and Qing, garden-builders, working in cities where space was limited, continued to build up earth and rockery hills as necessary landscape features. Rocks were used also as key elements of small courtyards, as cliffs, and as embankments of ponds. Rockery was regarded as the essential ingredient to set off and complement water, plants and architecture. Often sheer precipices and overhanging rocks were placed at the water's edge. Or, the straight line of cut stone revetments retaining a terrace in front of a hall or pavilion would contrast with an irregular shoreline of rocks and soil banks around a pond. Rockery hills also provided the higher elevations needed by garden 'travellers' for a broader view of the garden and of distant landscapes beyond the garden wall.

Viewed today, the most natural and evocative garden topography combines rockery hills with deep gullies, ravines and brooks which contrast with rugged peaks and ridges — the positioning of convex and concave forms to create a landscape that seems real and vibrant. Without such contrasts, the garden topography would appear dull and lifeless.

Hill Layout

In gardens with sufficient space to accommodate a pool, either the hill or the body of water is made the dominant feature. In all instances, however, the scale of one must seem to fit naturally into the other so that they both appear neither too imposing nor too insignificant. The height of a rockery hill built beside a pond is determined by the size of the pond, its water level, and the height of the banks on the far side. The higher the water level, the lower appears the hill. Likewise, where hills in larger gardens are built too close to each other, or where they almost completely surround a pond, the enclosed space will seem too cramped. Viewed from across a pond, the height and steepness of a hill is accentuated by cutting into its forward slope steps, terraces and gullies in irregular configurations.

The heights and sizes of buildings close to the edge of a garden pool also must relate in scale to the shape and height of the hill on the opposite side. The area around a pond would seem too sunken and stiff if it were encompassed on one side by a high hill and on the opposite side by high buildings. Constant concern for proper scale relationships precludes placing a tall building on a hill. Its very imposing presence would spoil the overall scale of the garden. On a high, steep hill, in particular, a pavilion should be set well below the summit so that the peak of the hill becomes the background for the building. And in all instances, the scale of the building must relate to the scale of the hill.

Looking from the garden to the hall, it is the architecture and its surrounding plantings that become the focus of interest when viewed from the hill. By contrast, high cliffs and rockery seen from the buildings produce an image of nature far freer than the straight lines of the architecture. To emphasise that difference, the highest point on the hill is kept out of a direct line with the central or most important room of the building.

Wherever hills are placed around a body of water, there must always be a breach in the higher topography — a low point or gap through which flows space, so that through the gap there is the suggestion of more distant vistas beyond the immediate highlands. In large gardens space may be subdivided by creating several hills of varying heights, some disposed laterally, and others in depth, as if they were a succession of peaks looming one behind the other as they recede into the distance. The effect is to increase perception of depth and the sense of the landscape's complexity and natural wildness.

Regardless of size, the relief of a hill's contours should be unmistakable, clear and distinct. Plantings should not obscure its profile. And to avoid a stiff, bilateral symmetry, a hill's highest point should be placed off-centre from the main viewing point. Rocks on the hill must be set to complement its topography, relating to its character, whether it has sharp peaks or gentle slopes. Rocks placed helter-skelter only convey an impression of disorder and triviality. The boring effect of a hill that is too flat can be rectified sometimes by the addition of a well-designed pavilion placed off-centre. To augment the hill's profile, compact evergreen shrubs of varying sizes may be massed on the slopes and summit of part of the hill. Ultimately, the landscape layout seems most natural and three-dimensional when the placement of its constituent features, such as peaks, cliffs, waterfalls, brooks, paths and bridges, complement each other to provide clear definition and contrasts.

Hills serve, as well, purposes other than aesthetic: they break down the overall amorphous garden space into more keenly grasped smaller spaces, reduce distracting and irritating extraneous noise, block blowing dust, and in summer help cool down the air temperature.

The magnitude and style of composition of rockery on a hill relates not only to the design effect sought, but also becomes simply a factor of the size of the area to be occupied and the hill's height. For example, a very high hill in a small space without rocks to retain its sides would be impossible to construct. Its steep slopes would soon collapse from either landslides or erosion. Thus, a high hill with no rocks must, of necessity, occupy a broad area. Save for very large gardens, such a hill would be totally out of scale. To build up high hills in small- to medium-sized gardens it is necessary, therefore, to use extensive rockery to create the effects of towering peaks and crags, as well as caves and ravines. It should be noted, however, that by the end of the Ming Dynasty, artists and garden lovers were warning against excessive use of rockery. One garden craftsman of the period, Zhang Lian, warned that 'a mass of peaks standing out against the sky' is less preferable than a 'low hill, gentle slope and uneven mounds (of earth) dotted with rocks.' In any event, the financial cost of rock work — both the material itself and its transportation and installation — also determines the quality and extent of rockery in a garden. But whether a man-made hill gets little or much rock work, the essential point is to make it look like a natural part of the landscape.

Rocky peaks and rugged mountain landscapes are represented either by extensive and intricate arrangements of rocks in many sizes disposed on a hill, or simply by an idealisation of rocky peaks in the symbolic form of a single standing rock, or tight grouping of several rocks, usually placed to be observed at closer range. Such symbolic peaks are found also at or near the centre of courtyards or other relatively confined spaces with buildings on several sides, so that the rocks, silhouetted against a wall, can be viewed from more than one angle.

On earthern hills rocks are disposed to appear as natural outcroppings. They bring to the landscape the sense of a deeper perspective, the look of a natural composition, that would be absent if rock arrangements were confined solely to shorelines, steps and peaks. Disposing of groupings in depth throughout the landscape creates the sense of nature rather than of a man-made terrain.

Precipitous rock-walled ravines and deep gullies play an especially evocative role in garden rockery. A narrow path will run along the bottom of a ravine. In the dark pass between two towering cliffs filters down only a thin ray of light from the patch of sky above. Often the silhouette of the overhanging branch of a twisted pine, holding on to the top of the cliff, or a single wild lily, can be seen from below. Such poignant contrasts between the massive weight and strength of rock and the delicacy of the pine branch or flower, or between the shadowy depths of the gorge and the light of the sky above, strikingly demonstrate the constant play of the duality of yin and yang.

Caves and grottoes also create contrasts of light and dark. Constructed in a rockery hill, they may form either one chamber or a zigzag tunnel-like space consisting of several connecting chambers of varying size. Wet caves are built at the base of a rock cliff overlooking a body of water. Since its floor is submerged, it can be entered only by boat.

The height and precipitous face of a cliff is emphasised by building a low, narrow, rock-studded path hugging the water's edge, or a zigzag bridge that crosses in front of it, almost touching the surface of the water. The path may penetrate into the face of the cliff, becoming a gully or gorge that winds its way up and through the hill until it reaches a terrace at or close to the summit.

Rock Types

There are basically two kinds of rock used in Chinese gardens: *tai-hu*

Figure 4.6: Huang-shi-tou
basaltic rocks *are the building
blocks forming peaks and cliffs
bordering a pebbly 'stream' of
mosaic pavement. Liu Yuan,
Suzhou.*

Figure 4.7: The mosaic pavements seem to flow around the compositions of tai-hu rocks and patches of mondo grass. Wang Shi Yuan and Yi Yuan, Suzhou.

and *huang-shi*. The term *tai-hu* denotes the furrowed and pierced limestone rock, in colours of off-white, bluish-white, gradations of grey, and black. The most renowned and prized rock is taken from the bed of Lake Tai (*tai-hu*), as well as from other lakes in central and south China. Equally prized are fanciful limestone rocks, riddled with holes, discovered in mountainous terrain. Found along stream beds, they have been eroded into their present convoluted forms by the harder gravels and sands impelled in the streams' swift currents. Others, dug from the earth, have had to be carefully cleansed of the brown and red soils in which they had lain, before their striking features could be uncovered.

Advising garden-builders on garden rockery, Ji Cheng, in *Yuan Ye*, his manual of landscape gardening, published in 1634, wrote that 'rocks exposed to weather and wind become old, but those which are taken up out the earth seem new. They are covered with earth. But if this is washed away by rain, and the stones exposed to the air, they too will assume an appearance of age.' *Yuan Ye* suggests further that 'if one wishes to produce something beautiful, one must not content oneself with the merely ornamental; the finished work must also be simple and all of a piece. If something lasting is wanted, strong, old stones should be used. But first attention must be paid to the nature and shape of the stones.'

The most imposing and well-shaped of these limestone rocks were often erected as a vertical monolith with more weight above than below. Tapering downward and widening upward, such a rock appears, nonetheless, well balanced like a dancer, arms outflung, supported on one foot, in a perfect state of equilibrium. At times it seems even like a lighter-than-air balloon, tugging at its tenuous moorings, straining to break away and soar up into the heavens. *Yuan Ye* prescribes that such rocks be set up in courtyards before big halls where they can be silhouetted against the white garden wall. They may be placed also out in the garden 'under a stately pine, combined with flowers ... or be used as a mountain ... where they will produce a magnificent effect.' Such standing *tai-hu* rocks function as abstract sculpture that, in contrast with works in galleries and gardens in the West, not only merge their amorphous shapes into the natural environment of plants and rugged topography, but also hold the capacity to evoke the grandeur and wild remoteness of mountains in nature.

Where *tai-hu* rockeries are placed to evoke memories of mountains, they fit naturally into the garden landscape. But where they are used to represent the bizarre, particularly to resemble animals and human figures, they appear strange and fantastic, and consequently are apt to introduce a discordant or distracting note into the otherwise natural unity of the landscape.

Within the category of *tai-hu* rocks garden-builders recognise differences in the kinds of surfaces: ridges and grooves that are vertical (like stalactites), horizontal or oblique striations, holes that are round or angular, and the shallow concave and convex surfaces that resemble eddy-like impressions left by retreating tides in the sandy

shallows of a beach. With such evocative textures in mind, the rockeries along the water's edge, for example, are composed of rocks selected to appear, when joined together, as a natural cliff or precipice, scoured and indented by the erosive lash of waves. Normally, the rocks are fitted together so that the joints are not noticeable, and, so that a rock set forward masks the joints of other rocks set behind it.

The second basic type of garden rock, *huang-shi* (yellow rock) is of basaltic origin, naturally fracturing into blocks of varying sizes, with irregular surfaces, tan and buff coloured, that run at both right and oblique angles. A good example of basaltic *huang-shi* in the United States is the rock composing The Palisades on the west bank of the lower Hudson River. In Chinese gardens *huang-shi* stone is used to form peaks, precipices, ravines, grottoes, and along shorelines to retain banks. It is not used, however, as a substitute for *tai-hu* rock, where use of the latter's twisted and furrowed forms are considered appropriate. Granite boulders, however, are used here and there to supplement basaltic stone. Their simple, uncomplicated forms do not seem unnatural or out of place when mixed with the blocky masses of basaltic *huang-shi* rockery. But unfitting is the mixing in the same composition of the light grey of the limestone *tai-hu* rocks with *huang-shi* rock. Their shapes and colours do not blend well, and in nature they are not found together.

A rockery slope of *huang-shi* looks especially natural where the blocks are randomly set to create the effect of stepped stone platforms, or tall stepping-stones. Though uneven, it is saved from chaos by the perpendicularity of their exposed facets: the tops of the 'stepping-stones' are held generally level, and each vertical face is set approximately plumb. Despite its overall irregularity and look of having been roughly strewn, it retains a sense of order and stability.

Figure 4.8: The distance seems foreshortened when one looks from one height across an abyss to another high point on the opposite side. Yi Yuan, Suzhou.

Rockery Construction

The designer of rockery exercises both aesthetic sensibility and engineering techniques, as well as an understanding of the qualities of each type of rock material at hand. Sketches, detailed drawings, and, at times, even scale models, precede the actual construction. Once construction commences, the designer-builder is in continual attendance supervising rock placement, from the smallest to the most massive. In selecting the best 'face' of each rock, taken into account are such factors as scale, shape, veining, colour and relationships to adjoining rock forms. Successful rock composition, consequently, requires adequate time and patience. And, as the work progresses, the designer does not hesitate to make changes and readjustments that he considers beneficial to the success of the work. In all rockery projects, of course, the safety and security of the construction is a constant consideration. The stones must rest on solid subsurface footings and foundations. In some cases, especially at the water's edge where the ground may be mushy, underwater pilings may have to be sunk before the rock work is begun.

There are two systems of rockery construction: one is the 'piling up' of rocks, one on top of the other, with their long axes kept perpendicular to the force of gravity. The second method is to hold the long axes of large rocks and boulders vertical, more or less parallel to gravitational pull. In the latter case the centre of gravity of each rock is balanced backwards and down so that its weight rests slightly back into the hillside, rather than forward into a downhill inclination. In this way there is no danger of rocks tipping over during the course of time as the ground shifts or settles. Whether set horizontally or vertically, however, both large and small rocks are composed in arrangements suggesting configurations found in nature.

Steps in the side of a rockery hill are built of the same type of rock

Figure 4.9: Its very height and mass cause the tai-hu monolith to dominate its bland surroundings. And the obvious biomorphic shape only adds to its vigour and force as a punctuation mark at the end of the paved walk. Liu Yuan, Suzhou.

used elsewhere on the hill so that, together, they appear as one unified mass. The tread and riser ratio may vary slightly from step to step, but not to the extreme that they become hazardous. The best relationship is six-inch riser with sixteen-inch tread. Varying the length of steps enhances the natural look of the construction. The cheek wall on the downhill side is composed of stout and stubby boulders. Thin or pointed stones are avoided. The boulders on each side of the steps, both at the bottom starting point and at the top, are never of equal height or girth. Along the way, intermediate turning points are also marked by boulders larger than the other cheek rocks. Hills, mainly composed of soil, use rocks and boulders as cheek walls irregularly set into the uphill side so that the steps appear to have depth, and thus look well integrated with the rest of the hill's rock compositions. This prevents the steps from looking as if they were tacked on to the hillside as an afterthought, rather than as a natural outcropping.

To provide strength of construction, the rocks in a grotto or cave are generally laid with their long axes horizontal, though the entry opening may be formed by vertical rocks on both sides, with a long rectangular slab set horizontally on top as the lintel — in effect, post and beam construction. To admit additional light and air into the grotto, crevices are left in the rock walls and roof.

Where rocks project from the face of a cliff, with their centre of gravity downhill, to convey a fearful aspect of overhanging precipices, they are set on a solid fulcrum of rock beneath, and then pinned down by a heavier rock above as a counterweight. Since metals rust or corrode, no dependence is ever placed upon metal ties, rods, hooks, pins, bars or straps to hold a rock in place. A mortar grout (cement and sand) is used only to fill in the joints between closely butted rocks. Before modern times, however, jointing grout

Figure 4.10: Stony path squeezed in a narrow defile of cliffs of tai-hu *rocks that rear up like two formless monsters waiting to pounce upon the unwary traveller. Liu Yuan, Suzhou.*

for *tai-hu* rocks consisted of mixtures, in varying proportions, of thin glutinous rice gruel, lime, tung oil, hemp fibre, and *qing-mei* (bluecoal dust). After pointing up the joints, a mixture of bittern and iron filings was daubed over the joints to hide the cracks. (Bittern is the mother liquor that remains in salt works after the salt has crystallised out.) To point up *huang-shi* rock, a mixture of *guang-jiao* (shiny glue), *qing-mei* and *yi-xing* (loess earth) was used. Today, pigmented mortar is used to fill joints. Generally, the joints between *tai-hu* rocks are made as indistinct as possible, while those between *huang-shi* rocks may be left more visible. The filler in their joints is raked or depressed to create a shadow line that distinctly defines the form of each rock.

Concluding his counsel on rockery, the author of *Yuan Ye* pertinently observed that although rocks and scholar-gardeners may be found here and there, the man who knows how to select rocks and to use them in a garden is rare. Three hundred years later, Osvald Siren, in his book *Gardens of China*, succinctly stated the importance of the designer's artistry: in 'creating works of art, the man is of greater importance than the material, however valuable that may be.'

Architecture

The pervasive reach of architecture throughout the Chinese classical garden, can seem at once to tip the balance in favour of art over nature. Yet this does not happen, for, in truth, the buildings, standing alone, would be out of context, paltry and meaningless were they disengaged from nature's hills, streams, pools, rocks and plants which they surround, leap over and penetrate. There is, of course, reciprocity at work here: while nature is being invaded by buildings, it, in turn, shows up, without fail, in the most architectural of spaces. The clearest and most ubiquitous example is the planting of trees and rockeries in the narrow, residual, odd-shaped spaces formed where *lang* galleries run parallel or at odd angles alongside walls and between the buildings they link.

The fusion of nature and architecture in a garden inevitably occurs where it serves the needs of both physical function and the user's spiritual and aesthetic goals and values. The insertion of buildings into the garden projects people painlessly into close contact with

Figure 4.11: The mirror image on the water is a calculated and essential element of this part of the garden. Zhuo Zheng Yuan, Suzhou.

Figure 4.12: The covered gallery provides a sheltered vantage point for viewing the lotus blossoms during the summer rains. Zhuo Zheng Yuan, Suzhou.

nature. And, as in the framing of a painting, windows, doorways and other apertures compose the view of the landscaped scene for the spectator. But the garden 'traveller' is not restricted to vistas seen only from buildings. There is also the pleasure of positioning himself outside, in the open, away from the confines of doorways and windows, to view at a distance the artful compositions of diverse architectural works tucked into the garden's natural landscape. Architecture has come to occupy between fifteen and thirty per cent of the total space in Chinese classical gardens — an indication of its importance.

Figure 4.13: Covered galleries or breezeways (lang) wind their zigzag ways, hugging walls or striking out into the open spaces of the garden, but never, in advance, revealing their ultimate destinations. Small pockets are created which are often planted with bamboo or other light-foliaged plants. Their leaves in the sunlight shine with a luminosity that sharply contrasts with the darker walkway and the shadowy ceiling. Zhuo Zheng Yuan and Wang Shi Yuan, Suzhou.

Architecture also plays a powerful role in the forming of recognisable landscape analogies — paired, equivalent or matched scenes — a unique characteristic of classical garden design. Throughout the garden are sensed relationships, aspects in common between nearby buildings and those viewed at a distance. Thus, for example, seated in a poolside *ting* pavilion, one gazes across the water and perceives on a distant hillside another *ting* pavilion. The shape and siting of a particular work of architecture may vary, but its repetition in the landscape creates a strongly felt unity. Similarly, such correspondences are sensed between natural features, such as groups of pines or flowering trees observed first in the foreground and then on a distant hillside.

The architecture within the garden provides also the windows, doorways and columns — in both curved and straight lines — to 'frame' the views of 'borrowed scenery' — an evocative outside landscape viewed from within the garden. It may be a natural feature, a pagoda, or a rude peasant hut on a distant hill. Or it can be an object close by, just outside the garden wall.

Depending upon the conditions of the site and their intended use, buildings assume a variety of shapes and sizes. A viewing pavilion, for instance, is designed and sited to afford the best view of seasonal

Figure 4.14: Typically, the ting is located below the summit of the hill, and is lightly screened by trees and shrubs to give it partial seclusion. From the bridge it is barely visible. As one progresses through the garden, a building may briefly appear in the distance, then for a time disappear before it is finally rediscovered when one is almost upon it. Zhuo Zheng Yuan, Suzhou.

phenomena. The way a building may be used in winter, spring, summer or fall is carefully considered in order to take advantage of the view of spring rain falling on a pond, a plum tree in blossom, falling snow on rocks, or a maple's scarlet leaves in autumn. The design and siting of garden buildings is also influenced by the shape and height of existing trees, especially those that are old and retain their interesting branching structure. One strives for compositions where each enhances the other.

Heightening the recognition of relationships between natural and man-made elements is the sense of clear, open and limitless space felt within garden architecture. The air of the garden and that of the building's interior become one. This melding of interior and exterior space is achieved by the creation of large and small courtyards, open, galleried corridors, doorways without doors, windows with only the tracery of open latticework. Such architectural means create separations between spaces while, at the same time establishing connections from building to building, and between building and nature. It makes inner and outer spaces run into each other, and evokes a sense of boundlessness.

The quality of infinite space is enhanced by the colouring of garden architecture. Generally, masonry walls are white, the roof tiles

Figure 4.15: The play of light and dark, repeated over and over again, is created by various intensities of light reflected off the white stucco walls. A characteristic of Chinese garden architecture is to refrain from extending the roof cover of the lang sheltered breezeway up to the walls, but instead to leave a gap so that light strikes the white wall from top to bottom. Then, not only is enough light admitted to promote plant growth, but it also becomes a luminous background to silhouette the graceful outlines of trees and shrubs, another example of Yin and Yang at work. Shrubs in pots and tubs supplement the permanently installed trees and shrubs. Here the shrubs are azalea, Japanese aucuba, a palm, a minor deciduous tree, and ubiquitous mondo grass around a composition of small rocks. The plant stand and garden seats are in carved marble. The courtyard pavement is a mosaic of stone chips, formed in the stylised plum blossom pattern repeated over a square grid. Yi Yuan, Suzhou.

black, and wood curtain partitions, columns, beams and railings a rich chestnut brown. White-washed walls serve not only as a light, contrasting background to silhouette both buildings, rockery and plants, and their shifting shadows, but also, in early morning mists, their pale surfaces seem to merge into the atmosphere. It is often impossible to differentiate the material background from the ethereal.

The names of most building types derive from their functions and forms. Regional differences in nomenclature, however, cause even experts to disagree on precise terminology. Those commonly accepted in Suzhou, the centre of the classical garden building tradition, are:

Figure 4.16: Like a giant snake, the lang (covered gallery) with its grey tile roof winds and zigzags its way through the garden. It is an all-weather passageway. The shrub at the lower right is Japanese aucuba. Zhuo Zheng Yuan, Suzhou.

The hall, termed *tang* when the roof beam is constructed of cylindrical timber, and *ting* when it is rectangular. Large halls, *da ting*, are sizable, pillared and lofty buildings, and generally the dominant architectural structure of the garden. As the owner's living quarters, or as his principal and most formal accommodation for receiving and entertaining guests, the *da ting* may cover floor space for as many as five rooms. It is usually connected by open galleries to subsidiary buildings, and its surrounding outdoor space may, in part, be walled off on one or two sides to form large landscaped courtyards. A *da ting* may be open on all sides, and if there are no nearby confining garden walls, by simply turning one's head, one may see, past open louvered doors, 360 degrees of a landscape panorama. Or, the gardens may be observed from outside while strolling along verandas that encompass the building. Subsidiary or attached to a *tang* or *da ting* may be a small room with windows (*xuan*) or guest accommodation (*guan*).

Smaller than a *da ting* are two other types of garden structures: one, *lou*, a storeyed building, and *ge*, a type of pavilion. Both *lou* and *ge* are usually two storeys high, the top storey's height being about 70 per cent of the height of the first floor's walls. A *lou* contains from one to five rooms; a *ge* has a smaller floor space. The second storey of both *lou* and *ge* has always less area than the lower rooms. To impart a dynamic look to the building, the lower storey's walls are usually white-washed plaster, while the second storey is, wholly or in part, built of wood. A *ge* generally has double eaves, and, for a light and airy look, is built with windows on all sides. Its plan is a square, or polygon of more than four sides, and whether of one or two storeys, it is still considered a *ge*. When a *ge* is built half in water and half on land it is called a *xie*. The water side is open and without a railing.

Figure 4.17: Though the courtyard is small, the rockery has the power to stir the imagination to see far-off mountain peaks. The plain stucco walls become the 'sky' stretching into infinity behind the profile of the rocky horizon. Wang Shi Yuan, Suzhou.

Figure 4.18: The round gateway and the billowing rhythm of the wall bring to the scene a strong sense of movement and dynamism. Yi Yuan, Suzhou.

Figure 4.19: The feeling of total enclosure in a narrow space is moderated by the opening provided by the latticed window. It is softened further by the clump of bamboo and the wisteria climbing along the tiles of the wall coping, as if to connect up the interior to the outside world. By opening on to such small enclosures, the room gets natural light yet preserves its seclusion. The carved wooden shutters can swivel back for more privacy. Yi Yuan, Suzhou.

Figure 4.20: The silhouette of a tree is enough to introduce a sense of life into this tiny space open to the sky. Wang Shi Yuan, Suzhou.

Figure 4.22: In Chinese houses, access to the outdoors through courtyards, large or small, assures adequate air circulation and daylight. The opportunity is never lost to introduce forms of nature, no matter how sparse, even in the most restricted spaces. Here, it is low rockery, a rambling espaliered rose bush against the wall, and mondo grass. The floor is a chequerboard mosaic of white pebbles and grey stone shards. The doors are carved wood. Wang Shi Yuan, Suzhou.

Figure 4.21: Although it is simply a partly covered passageway linking one courtyard with another, thought was given, even in this small space, to suggesting a mountain scene of rocky peaks with a spindly nandina representing mountain foliage. The trunk of the ivy seems to grow out of the rock and wall, and, in its bold, sweeping curve ties the roof to the ground. The elongated octagon of an opening in the wall is in perfect scale with the space. The four-character plaque, suggesting the feeling of its setting, reads: 'LI BU XIAO ZHU (Linger in this humble room). Liu Yuan, Suzhou.

Figure 4.23: The round form of the so-called 'moon gate' effectively frames the scene on the other side of the wall. It works in both directions. Yi Yuan, Suzhou; Shi Zi Lin, Suzhou; Cang Lang Ting, Suzhou and 'Pi Ba Yuan (Loquat Garden)', Zhuo Zheng Yuan, Suzhou.

The small pavilion, kiosk or gazebo located in out-of-the-way parts of the garden is called a *ting*. (The Chinese character for *ting* [pavilion] is completely different from *ting* [hall].) Because of its intimate size, there is more flexibility in the siting of the *ting* pavilion in garden locations too precarious and difficult for larger structures. In effect, the *ting* is a summer house (in Japanese, *azumaya*), arbor or bower, often secluded, but also a vantage point for observing phenomena of nature, distant garden views, and even a place of escape from the 'crowd'. The *ting* may be set either on a hillside, hidden within a grove of trees or bamboo, on the banks of a pond, or by a garden path. And, although, in one sense, a sheltered retreat, from an opposite point of view a *ting* may be also a focus of interest embellishing a remote part of the landscape observed from the main room

Figure 4.24: *The wall forms a well-defined barrier between the grey tai-hu rocks in the foreground and the chunky tan basaltic rocks on the far side of the moon gate. The two types of rock are never mixed together in the same rockery arrangement. The tree on the left is loquat. Mondo grass and dwarf bamboo are clumped where rockery meets pavement. Zhuo Zheng Yuan, Suzhou.*

of a *da ting* hall. Conditions of a particular site determine the size and shape of a *ting*. But whether high on a hill or by a pond, it is always tucked in among trees and shrubs to tie it in with surrounding natural features of the landscapes.

There are two kinds of *ting*: attached and free-standing. The attached *ting* is connected to other structures by a *lang* corridor. Or, it may be built on to a wall to form a *ban-ting* (half pavilion) within a courtyard. A recent example in the West of a *ban-ting* is in the Hall of Staying Spring courtyard of Wang Shi Yuan (Fisherman's Net Garden) reproduced in adapted form in the Metropolitan Museum of Art, New York City.

The free-standing *ting*, isolated from other architectural structures, depends solely upon its own position in the midst of nature for its interest and charm. In plan, a *ting* may assume a variety of shapes: square, rectangle, hexagon, octagon, circle, fan, plum blossom or other floral forms. A single-eaved roof is more common than a roof with double eaves. A square *ting* with single eaves has four or twelve columns; a hexagonal *ting* has six columns; and an octagonal *ting* has eight columns. The height of a column in a square *ting* commonly is eight-tenths of the distance between parallel sides. In a hexagonal *ting* it is ten-fifteenths; and in an octagon, ten-sixteenths. The diameter of a column is one-tenth of its length. A free-standing *ting* is open on all sides, save for a low sitting wall with stone or tile coping and leaning balustrade set between the columns.

Figure 4.25: Oval doorway framed by moulding of baked clay. The flowing curve of the low retaining wall edging along the planting bed is repeated in the coping of the garden wall in the background. Du Fu's Cottage, Chengdu.

Figure 4.26: Doorways in recognisable shapes, accentuated by contrasts of light and shadow, become well-defined elements of a garden's design. Cang Lang Ting, Suzhou; Zhuo Zheng Yuan, Suzhou and Yu Yuan, Shanghai.

Figure 4.27: There is a progression of levels of light from the foreground's dark doorway through the intermediate intensity on the vase-shaped portal to the sunny brightness of the rockery outside. This hierarchy of luminosity evokes a sense of order and anticipation. Summer Palace, Beijing.

Figure 4.28: The shadowy formation of dark rock is framed in the curving white aperture. The stark contrast of light and dark enhances a sense of mystery. Shi Zi Lin, Suzhou.

Figure 4.29: The octagon gate frames the view beyond of a massive rock, as if it were a giant creature poised to pounce upon, or embrace, the next wanderer who passes through the opening. Shi Zi Lin, Suzhou.

Figure 4.30: Doorway in the conventionalised four-lobed plum blossom figure. The door frame is ceramic tile. The plaque over the doorway reads: 'Tan Yu (Search For Serenity)'. Shi Zi Lin, Suzhou.

Linking up various elements of the garden is the *lang* (open gallery or corridor). It serves both as a sheltered connector route through parts of the garden between buildings and as a guide that leads the spectator over meandering paths through shifting landscape scenes. It also helps to enhance the perception of horizontal depth by compartmentalising the overall space.

Built in many forms, the *lang* can be straight, zigzag, or undulating, and may run along direct or circuitous routes on flat or hilly terrain, along ponds and pools, or, like a causeway or long bridge, leap across the water. The *qu lang*, true to its zigzag configuration, winds through the garden, directing the eye of the 'traveller' to and fro, towards a succession of views as he passes along. One end of a *qu lang* leads off a wall, and as it takes its zigzag, in-and-out course, alongside but out from a garden wall, it forms a series of small yards which become perfect settings for abstract landscapes of rocks and plants.

The *fu lang* is a dual *lang*: two covered corridors separated by a common wall pierced by many fancifully latticed window openings. Although the wall separates one part of the garden from the other, its latticed windows present glimpses, as one moves along, of different views of the garden on the other side. One is impressed with expectations of scenes yet to be encountered.

Where the need is felt for a sheltered garden corridor, obstacles of difficult garden topography seem easily overcome. Undulating *lang*, termed *pa shan lang*, following the terrain, march up and down hills. At the water's edge, like a stretched-out dragon, a *lang* extends itself over a pond, forming an elongated covered bridge, called *shui lang*. By cutting over the water, it makes the spaces on both sides seem larger.

Whatever its shape, configuration or disposition, the *lang* always appears light and graceful. It must never look too high or wide. Width across is from four to five feet; distance between columns is approximately nine to ten feet; column diameter about six inches; and height of columns approximately eight feet.

Courtyards

The distinct character of a Chinese classical garden derives not only from the mass of its architectural elements — wooden buildings, and tile-capped masonry walls — but just as formative and unique are the spaces that they enclose: its courtyards, integral and intimate extensions of the structures themselves. The quality of light and shade in a courtyard, the awareness of space that it stimulates, the subtle compositions of its rockeries and plantings that evoke images of distant landscapes, the playful originality of window shapes and latticework, and the artful patterns of mosaic pavements combine to create an overwhelming sense of fitness and tranquillity. More than any other feature of the garden, the courtyard consistently expresses a unique form that is timely and adaptable for contemporary residential design in the West.

In China the courtyard developed out of the need to get the most

Figure 4.31: The window grillework is ceramic. The opening on the right is the pomegranate motif; on the left, peony. Cang Lang Ting, Suzhou.

Figure 4.32: The ingenuity of elaboration extends from the tiling on the roof and eaves to the intricate tracery in the windows, and the flame and leaf motif of the doorway. Yet there is an intimate fusion with nature in the supporting rockery which pushes up into the low sitting wall. Shi Zi Lin, Suzhou.

out of limited available space. It had to satisfy both mundane functional needs as well as the owner's aesthetic aspirations. Courtyards provided much-needed privacy from the outside world, and, at the same time, with its rockeries and plantings, introduced a sense of the landscapes of nature beyond its walls.

Changes over the centuries in functional requirements and architectural styles have created three basic types of enclosed garden spaces adjacent to buildings. One is the courtyard formed by three white-washed walls and the front or back of a building. Aside from the courtyard's ground plane, used for rockeries, trees and shrubs, or for terraces with annual and perennial flowers, the rest of the surface is paved with bricks or mosaics of pebble and tile. While the edging of

the paved area abutting the building or the courtyard's walls follows the straight lines at its base, the paving that runs into the rocks and plantings follows the ins and outs of their irregular configurations.

A second form of enclosed space is both the small yard formed between a building and a *lang* corridor, as well as the tiny walled-in space formed to give both light, ventilation and privacy to back rooms which do not face the garden. Generally, such spaces are intended to be entered only for purposes of maintenance and are therefore not paved. Instead, they are planted with one or more trees or shrubs, such as nandina, wintersweet, banana, or bamboo. In addition, one or more *tai-hu* lake rocks may be set to stand in the narrow space, projecting up into view just outside the room's windows. Together with plantings, they make the space seem bigger. In a sense, these narrow ventilator light wells become life-size versions of miniature potted landscapes.

A third form is a complex courtyard that combines elements of the first and second categories. It has a large main courtyard with a rockery feature and plantings in the centre surrounded by pavements. The main courtyard is, in turn, bounded, not by walls but by open *lang* corridors. The spaces on the outer sides of each leg of the open corridors form small side yards noted above as the second type of courtyard. From whatever orientation within this complex courtyard one perceives any single feature through an expanded depth of field

Figure 4.33: Unglazed windows in a garden wall framed by mouldings of baked clay painted black. One is shaped like a fan; the other simply a symmetrical curved figure. The views of trees and foliage on the other side of the wall compose an intricate, lacy 'chiaroscuro'. Du Fu's Cottage, Chengdu.

Figure 4.34: Window grillework patterns are never repeated in the same wall. The ceramic traceries admit air and light, and prevent the feeling of being completely closed in. They introduce the strong perception of human artistry on to the plain 'canvas' of the white stucco-faced wall. Zhuo Zheng Yuan, Suzhou; Yu Yuan, Shanghai.

formed by a series of vertical planes of columns, eaves, rocks, trees, walls and windows. Despite the existence of the outer enclosing walls, the effect from within is one of infinite space.

The garden walls of any of the aforementioned types of enclosed spaces, for maximum privacy and quiet, may be entirely blank, or for admission of a greater sense of space beyond, may be pierced with window openings, either latticed or ungrilled. Windowed walls permit air to circulate more freely, light and sound to enter, and offer tantalising visual contact with the landscape on the other side. The effect is to enhance a sense of openness despite the walled enclosure of the space.

Finally, there are larger garden spaces, not courtyards, but rather the expanses segregated by a complex of houses, garden walls, corridors, rockeries, hills, copses of trees and bodies of water. The several spaces formed by configurations of these elements become irregular and intricate, and are the most suggestive of purely natural landscapes. The ground is mostly occupied by plantings and rockery. Pavements are kept to paths and the floors of buildings.

Figure 4.35: The constant interplay of light and shadow in a Chinese garden: walls, alternating from light to shadow, have apertures that alternate in reverse. It is the pervasive demonstration of the duality of Yin and Yang. Yi Yuan, Suzhou.

Figure 4.36: Changes in grade may be accommodated by making steps of natural stone which become an architectural feature, yet in a natural form and material — a linking element between cut stone slabs and pebbles and fieldstone. Yu Yuan, Shanghai and Wang Shi Yuan, Suzhou.

Figure 4.37: Mosaic pavement under construction: Base course is gravel. Setting bed: sand. The conventionalised plum blossom pattern is formed by curved tile sections set on edge. Pebbles of different shades are set by hand into the spaces defined by the tiles. Bricks form the straight lines of the edging. Finally, a mixture of dry sand, stone dust and a small amount of dry cement is swept into the crevices, and then lightly wetted down with a gentle spray of water. Nanjing.

Figure 4.38: Cast-iron catch basin grating. Diao Yutai, Beijing.

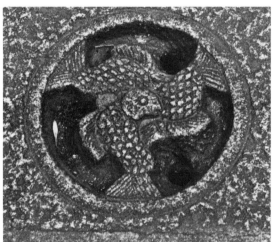

Figure 4.39: Garden pavement drain inlets with stone covers carved into conventional geometrical and animal figures — all symbols of good fortune. Yu Yuan, Shanghai.

Figure 4.40: The drain grating is of carved granite in the Chinese cash motif of interlocked coins, the symbol of prosperity. Yu Yuan, Shanghai.

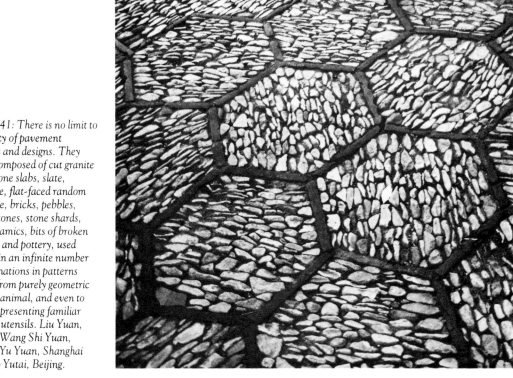

Figure 4.41: There is no limit to the variety of pavement materials and designs. They may be composed of cut granite or limestone slabs, slate, sandstone, flat-faced random field stone, bricks, pebbles, broken stones, stone shards, glass, ceramics, bits of broken dishware and pottery, used alone or in an infinite number of combinations in patterns ranging from purely geometric to floral, animal, and even to shapes representing familiar domestic utensils. Liu Yuan, Suzhou; Wang Shi Yuan, Suzhou; Yu Yuan, Shanghai and Diao Yutai, Beijing.

Plants

The rain drops of the night, which fall upon the banana leaves, are like the tears of the weeping mermaid (pearls). When the morning breeze flows through the willows, the latter bend like the slender waists of dancing girls.

Before the window one plants bamboo, and between the courtyards pear trees. The moonlight lies like glittering water over the countryside. The wind sighs in the trees and gently touches the lute and the book that lie on the couch. The dark, rippled mirror of water swallows the half moon. When day dawns one is awakened by the fresh breeze; it reaches the bed, and all the dust of the world is blown out of one's mind.

Such is the intense poetic expression in *Yuan Ye* of the traditional association in the Chinese mind between trees and flowers and the myriad phenomena of nature and human experience.

The great land mass of China was relatively unaffected by the Pleistocene glaciations which destroyed so many plant species in North America and Europe. It encompasses a wide range of landscapes and climates: steaming jungles and arid northern wastes; rugged, forested mountains, broad river valleys and watery coastal

Figure 4.42: Waterlilies growing in a pottery bowl in a garden courtyard. Wang Shi Yuan, Suzhou.

plains. Such diverse environments, with the rich palette of plants which they have engendered, have, from earliest times, inspired garden-builders. Such inspiration is revealed both in the characteristic moulding of the classical garden's ground plane and in the always apt choice of plant species faultlessly disposed throughout each sector of the garden. All such exemplary garden landscapes are founded upon an asymmetrical plan of heights and dips, earth and water, and a basic planting composition of trees, woody shrubs, bamboo clumps, and herbaceous material that preserve their form or reappear through all seasons.

Figure 4.43: Tray landscape in a cut stone tub. Surrounded by water, the rocks appear as islands in a fantasy landscape inspired by a famous painting. Du Fu's Garden, Chengdu.

The plants of a Chinese garden play not only their obvious roles as constituent elements, but also, through their traditional symbolic and historic associations, set mood, theme and character of each section of the garden. They may even decide the names of garden buildings: Yuan Xiang Tang (Distant Fragrance Hall), Xue Xiang Yun Wei Ting (Snow Fragrance Blue Cloud Pavilion), or Song Feng Ting (Pine Wind Pavilion).

While the plant compositions in some garden settings depend upon the predominance of foliage plants, in other sectors flowering plants, changing from month to month, form the seasonal character of a particular area. For example, magnolias planted in front of a pavilion, or peonies on a raised flower terrace serve mainly as an expression of springtime. Copses of blooming crape myrtle trees or lotus plants in ponds are manifestations of summer. A forest of maple trees in flaming foliage, chrysanthemums and sweet-scented osmanthus form an autumn display. And camellias, red-berried nandina,

Figure 4.44: Dwarfed trident maple trees placed in conspicuous areas of the garden. The Chinese term for dwarfed plants is penjing (bonsai in Japanese). Yu Yuan, Shanghai.

wintersweet and winterberry indicate a winter scene. In some sections of a garden flowering trees, shrubs and herbaceous plants from each blooming period are planted so that throughout the year there is no lack of colour as the landscape undergoes seasonal changes.

As in gardens elsewhere, the choice of plants for a particular part of a Chinese garden is influenced also by topography, soil moisture, soil type, prevailing winds, temperatures, and the habit and ultimate size of the plant. Thus, at the corner of a building, where there is shade, and where it is easy to bring water to plants, sweet-scented

Figure 4.45: The gnarled trunks of the wisteria vine supported by the simple pergola, convey a sense of age and the continuity of life. It appears to be growing from the rocks which anchor the vine to the ground. The sinuous shape and sparseness of the vine are the result of assiduous and faithful pruning. The vine provides not only a shady resting place but also a focal point of interest, especially during its period of blooming, April and May. Xi Yuan, Suzhou.

osmanthus, camellias, Chinese littleleaf box, nandina, Chinese holly and glossy privet may be planted. On hilly areas farther from the house, larger, more drought-resistant plants, such as pine, elm, jujube and yucca may be placed. Similarly, damp-soil plants, such as willow, pterocarya, and pomegranate are arranged at the edges of ponds. Of course, other equally important determining factors in plant composition are the line, mass, colour and even fragrance of the plants themselves. And existing large, old trees, by setting a mood of permanence and age, may become, themselves, the most important factors in determining the planting plan.

Plants frequently used in Chinese classical gardens may be grouped as follows:

Shade Trees

Evergreen: Yew Podocarpus, Lacebark Pine, Black Pine, Masson Pine, Hinoki Cypress, Sawara Cypress, Cryptomeria, Camphor Tree, Deodar Fir, Silk Oak Grevillea, Tanyosho Pine, Chinese Parasol Tree.

Deciduous: Ginkgo, Siberian Elm, Chinese Hackberry, Japanese Zelkova, Muku Tree, Chinese Scholar Tree, Chinese Toon, Chinaberry Tree, Silktree, Chinese Catalpa, Chinese Pistache, Chinese Honeylocust, Chinese Wingnut Tree, Chinese Ash, Oriental Plane Tree, Metasequoia, Weeping Willow.

Decorative Foliage Species

Evergreen: Chinese Littleleaf Box, Aucuba, Gold Dust, Japanese Cleyera, Sago Cycas, India Rubber Tree, Banana, Coral Ardisia, Cast Iron Plant, Japanese Aralia, Japanese Holly, Chinese Holly, Glossy Privet, Yucca, Palms, Kaizuca Juniper, Chinese Photinia, Japanese Pittosporum, Rhododendrons, Azaleas, Serissa, Leatherleaf Viburnum.

Deciduous: Japanese Maple, Chinese Tallow Tree, Chinese Tamarisk, Redleaf Plum, Chinese Abelia, Korean and Japanese Barberry, Smoketree, Japanese Enkianthus, Winged Spindletree, Chinese Witchhazel, Nandina, Korean Spice Viburnum.

Figure 4.46: The courtyard comes alive in late spring with the blooming of the ancient, twisted wisteria and the peonies in the raised, rock-retained bed on the left. Vines, such as wisteria, offer more than the two-dimensional effect produced when they simply cling to walls. Here, pruning and training over many years creates a picturesque shrub, which, when necessary, can be supported by a wooden crutch. Specimen flowering shrubs achieve greater importance when located close to the house from which they can be observed and appreciated in all weather and all seasons. Wang Shi Yuan, Suzhou.

Flowering Species

Evergreen: Japanese and Sasanqua Camellias, Sweet-scented Osmanthus, Yulan Magnolia, Rhododendrons, Oleander, Cape Jasmine, Chinese St Johnswort, Japanese Serissa, Sweet Viburnum, Fragrant Viburnum, Royal Jasmine, Banana Shrub.

Deciduous: Tree Peony, Star and Saucer Magnolias, Flowering Plum, Peach, Apricot, and Cherries, Flowering Crab apples, Crape Myrtle, Rose of Sharon, Wintersweet, Chinese Redbud, Bigleaf Hydrangea, White Old-fashioned Weigela, Winter Jasmine, Forsythia, Kerria, Flowering Almond, Flowering Quince.

Decorative Fruiting Species

Evergreen: Loquat, Tangerine, Citron, Chinese Holly, Nandina, Coral Ardisia, Sweet Viburnum.

Deciduous: Pomegranate, Crab apples, Persimmon, Fig, Jujube, Chinese Wolfberry, Quince.

Bamboos

Elephant Bamboo, Beechey Sinocalamus, Stone Bamboo, Indocalamus, Sassa Bamboo, Mottled Bamboo, Black Bamboo, Square Bamboo, Castillon Bamboo.

Herbaceous and Water Plants

Chrysanthemums, Plaintain Lily, Dwarf Lilyturf, Mondo Grass, Peony, Iris, Impatience Balsam, Narcissus, Day-lily, Orchids, Lotus, Waterlily, Phragmites.

How plants are composed in a garden — whether placed as solitary specimens, standing alone, or assembled as a group, in pure stands or a mixture of species — is determined by the design effect sought by the builder. Working out the planting plan requires consideration of the plant's size, shape, habit, foliage texture, density and colour, blossom colour, fragrance, blooming time, fruiting effect, its aspect in each season, how it relates to adjacent features, such as rockery, water surfaces and buildings, and, of course, its particular horticultural requirements. In Chinese classical gardens there is one further governing consideration: special emphasis is placed upon using plants in settings similar to their native natural environments. Thus, for example, if in nature willow trees or clumps of reeds are usually found around bodies of water, one would not plant them on the top of a hill. Conversely, dense bamboos will be found on a hillside, and a twisted, windblown pine would be planted among rocks on the garden's craggy hills, as if it were seen in nature on a high mountainside, and not in a low wetland. The essential aim is always to try to evoke in the mind of the beholder a sense of conformity with nature, or even of the wild, beyond the garden wall.

Equally important, however, is the play of elements of logic and practicality, which meet in any work of art that must also serve a functional purpose. In designing a planting for a small yard or confined space, for instance, a single tree by itself may have to sustain the design. Its importance is magnified, because only at close quarters can one appreciate the full effect of its habit, colour and fragrance. When a striking effect is sought, a tree or shrub of unusually expressive or exquisite habit may be planted as a single specimen at the

Figure 4.47: The Boston ivy creeps over parts of the rocky shoreline, linking the aquatic plant life of lotuses with the terrestial elements of trees and shrubs. Although the space is

corner of a building, at the end of a bridge, at the junction of paths, or at the bend in a stream or pond. Furthermore, if the plant repeats a species already encountered, or is paired with one visible in the distance, it injects an added sense of unity into the landscape by recapitulating what has passed and forecasting what is to come. At times the single specimen may be planted in front of a copse of trees or bamboo grove to enliven a backdrop which, by itself, may tend to be dull or monotonous. Such a ploy is successful when the texture or colour of the single specimen's foliage sharply contrasts with the background planting: for example, a magnolia or red-leafed plum placed in front of bamboo.

small, the high shrubs and rocks, concealing the routes of the paths, create a sense of mystery and infinite space which, in reality, is contained within the finite limits of the garden's perimeter walls. Zhuo Zheng Yuan, Suzhou.

In larger garden spaces, where trees of the same species are planted together to form a copse or clumps, the unique character of each species is underlined. A strong design statement is thus impressed upon the scene.

But the unique appeal of a species may not only derive from its habit or colouring, such as a grove of Japanese maples in October. One may also take into account the fragrance of it flowers or foliage, such as a grouping of apple trees, sweet-scented osmanthus in flower, a grove of pines or balsam firs.

Even mixed stands of deciduous and evergreen trees, often found in nature, may also create a pleasing natural landscape when placed in groups with enough room for each species to flourish, and where the total composition is planned so that each grouping is displayed for its best effect as seen from a main viewing point. Thus care is taken to ensure that lower-growing plants are not obscured by taller species, so that each receives its adequate share of sunlight. Contrast and definition of foliage textures are taken into account, making each specimen or grouping stand out as an individual design element unconfused with neighbouring plants.

Another advantage to planting groupings of evergreen trees with deciduous species is to enliven an often dull and monotonous winter landscape consisting only of deciduous material.

In smaller enclosed spaces, such as courtyards, and in the narrow earth beds between *lang* galleries and walls, the choice of plant material is constrained by considerations of scale and distances separating the observer from the plants. One must select plants that are effective when seen at close range because of their especially delicate and beautiful branching structures, colours or fragrances. Consideration is also given as to how they combine with adjacent rockery and the effect of their vibrating shadow patterns projected on the background of white-washed walls.

Commonly used plants in very small spaces are bamboo and banana. In somewhat larger spaces are planted yulan magnolia, sweet-scented osmanthus, crape myrtle, lacebark pine, shrubby yew podocarpus, Chinese littleleaf box, and Japanese maple. But whether large or small, constant attention is paid to pruning to keep the plants in scale with their confined spaces.

In addition to trees and shrubs, vines also play a role in both large and small courtyards to break up the expanse of white walls and to soften the possibly too pervasive impression of architecture and masonry. Typically used are Boston ivy, Chinese trumpet creeper, confederate jasmine, and several species of climbing roses.

The wide, open spaces of classical gardens, with their hills, rockeries, large ponds and pools, also contain stands of tall trees which, in part, establish the gardens' overall structure. They strengthen the composition by linking buildings to the terrain, the rockeries, and to other buildings. They form the visual dividing elements of the gardens' inner spaces. Among such major trees are camphor, cryptomeria, pines, gingko, cassia, oak, Chinese parasol tree, elm, maple, willow, ash, plane, sophora, and Chinese wingnut.

Figure 4.48: The bare white stucco wall is the perfect backdrop for emphasising the graceful lines of the multi-stemmed rose bush. Assiduous pruning keeps the plant in a semi-espalier form so that it does not encroach upon the path. The line of mondo grass along the bottom, separating the vertical masonry of the wall from the horizontal stonework of the path, relieves the heaviness of the two if joined at the bottom. The mondo grass also establishes a green horizontal base to anchor the verticality of the climbing rose. Wang Shi Yuan, Suzhou.

Plantings close to buildings are selected not only for their intrinsic features, such as fragrant blossoms or attractive habit, but thought is also given to how they enhance the architecture as it relates to the total composition of the garden. How, for example, does the white, mottled bark of the lacebark pine work with the dark brown wood of the adjoining *ting* pavilion. Care is also taken not to make plantings too dense around buildings so as not to hide their outlines or to prevent daylight from entering the building. For the same reason, only sparse plantings are made on the side of a building facing a pool or pond in order not to obscure the view of the water.

In all instances, however, whether a pavilion is on a hill or by the waterside, there must be some adjacent plantings to link the building with its surrounding landscape.

On garden hills without buildings, the sought-after effect of the illusion of a verdant mountain forest is achieved with plantings of both tall trees and understorey species, both deciduous and evergreen.

On hills where rock predominates, plantings, as in nature, are

Figure 4.49: The shadows of plants cast upon walls and pavements are dynamic elements of the garden's design. Liu Yuan, Suzhou.

sparse. Trees on cliffs overlooking water are often twisted pines, hackberry, or crape myrtle, whose branches are pruned to show their odd structures against a background of rocky cliffs and water.

Plantings on the banks of garden ponds are generally deciduous trees interspersed with low evergreen and deciduous shrubs. Pendent or overhanging shrubs, such as winter jasmine, are planted on very high embankments to diminish the impression of the extreme height. Care always is taken, however, not to plant too densely around ponds and garden lakes to prevent obstructing views of the water, islets and bridges.

Since the inverted reflections on a water surface of nearby rockery, pavilions, bridges and other features are important aspects of the garden landscape, no water plants, such as lotus or waterlily, are permitted where an expanse of clear water is required. Reeds and other discrete shore and marsh grasses, however, are planted where they enhance the feeling of wild nature along the shoreline. They also provide food and breeding places for fish living in the garden pond.

Chapter 5
Annotated Plant List

The trees, shrubs, vines, bamboos and herbaceous plants, listed here by their botanical and common English names, are generally cultivated in Europe and North America. Chinese names have been added only in those cases where there is general agreement by Chinese taxonomists on their nomenclature. Many not found in Chinese gardens are also included because they would be appropriate and attractive, and, in the author's opinion, if they were to be found in Chinese horticulture, they would be used. The Chinese names are shown in the official *pinyin* system of the People's Republic of China. The diacritical marks over the Chinese renditions represent the four main tones of the Mandarin dialect, the standard national language of China.

The list is divided into the following categories: major evergreen trees; major deciduous trees; minor evergreen trees; minor deciduous trees; evergreen shrubs; deciduous shrubs; vines; herbaceous and aquatic plants; bamboos.

Major Trees, Evergreen

Abies firma (Moma Fir) RÌBEN LĚNG SHĀN
Abies homolepis (Nikko Fir) RÌ GUĀNG LĚNG SHĀN
Abies koreana (Korean Fir) CHÁO XIĀN LĚNG SHĀN
Cedrus deodara (Deodar Fir) XUÈ SŌNG
Chamaecyparis lawsoniana (Lawson False Cypress) LÁO SHĒN HUĀ BÒ
Chamaecyparis obtusa (Hinoki False Cypress) RÌBEN BIǍN BÒ
Chamaecyparis pisifera (Sawara False Cypress) RÌBEN HUĀ BÒ
Chamaecyparis pisifera filifera (Thread Sawara Cypress) XIÀN BÒ
Chamaecyparis pisifera plumosa (Plume Sawara Cypress) FĒNG WĚI BÒ
Chamaecyparis pisifera squarrosa (Moss Sawara Cypress) RÓNG BÒ
Cinnamomum camphora (Camphor Tree) SHANG ZHÀN SHÙ
Cinnamomum cassia (Cassia Tree) ROÙ GUÌ
Cryptomeria japonica (Cryptomeria) RÌBEN LĬU SHĀN
Cunninghamia lanceolata (Common China Fir) SHĀN MÙ
Cupressus macrocarpa (Monterey Cypress) DǍ GǓO BÒ MÙ
Cupressus sempervirens stricta (Columnar Italian Cypress) ZHÙ XÍNG
     YÌDÀLÌ BÒ
Cupressus (Chamaecyparis) funebris (Mourning Cypress)
Cupressus torulosa (Himalaya Cypress) ZÀNG BÒ
Cupressus torulosa 'sushengbai' (Himalaya Cypress variety) SU SHENG
     BǍI
Grevillea robusta (Silk-oak Grevillea) YÍN HUÁ
Picea asperata (Dragon Spruce) YÚN SHĀN
Picea polita (Tigertail Spruce) HǓ WĚI YÚN SHĀN
Picea smithiana (Himalaya Spruce) XǏ MǍ YÚN SHĀN
Pinus bungeana (Lacebark Pine) BǍI PÍ SŌNG
Pinus densiflora (Japanese Red Pine) CHÌ SŌNG
Pinus densiflora oculus-draconis (Dragon's Eye Pine)
Pinus densiflora umbraculifera (Tanyosho Pine) PÍNG TÓU CHÌ SŌNG
Pinus koraiensis (Korean Pine) HǍI SŌNG

Pinus massoniana (Masson Pine) MǍ WĚI SŌNG
Pinus parviflora (Japanese White Pine) RÌBEN WǓ ZHĒN SŌNG
Pinus strobus (Eastern White Pine) MĚIGUÓ WǓ ZHĚN SŌNG
Pinus tabuliformis (Chinese Pine)
Pinus thunbergi (Japanese Black Pine) HĒI SŌNG
Podocarpus macrophylla (Yew Podocarpus) LUŌ HÀN SŌNG
Podocarpus macrophylla maki (Shrubby Yew Podocarpus) XIǍO YÈ LUŌ
    HÀN SŌNG
Podocarpus nagi (Japanese Podocarpus) JÚBǍI
Sterculia platanifolia (*Firmiana simplex*) (Chinese Parasol Tree) WU
    TUNG
Thuja occidentalis nigra (Dark American Arborvitae) XIĀNG BÒ
Thuja orientalis (Oriental Arborvitae) CÈ BǍI
Thuja standishii (Japanese Arborvitae) XIǍN BǍI
Thujopsis dolabrata (Hiba False Arborvitae) LǓO HÀN BÒ
Tsuga chinensis (Chinese Hemlock) TǏE SHĀN
Tsuga diversifolia (Japanese Hemlock) RÌBEN TǏE SHĀN
Tsuga yunnanensis (Yunnan Hemlock) YUNNAN TǏE SHĀN

Major Trees, Deciduous

Aesculus chinensis (Chinese Horse Chestnut) QÌ YÈ SHÙ
Ailanthus altissima (Tree of Heaven) CHÒU CHŪN
Albizzia julibrissin rosea (Hardy Silktree Albizzia) HÓNG HǍ HUǍN
Carpinus betulus (European Hornbeam) OŪZHOŪ É ĚR LÌ
Carpinus caroliniana (American Hornbeam) QIAN JǏN TÉNG
Castanea mollissima (Chinese Chestnut) BǍN LÌ
Celtis bungeana (Bunge Hackberry) XIǍO PÈ PǓ
Celtis sinensis (Chinese Hackberry) PǓ SHÙ
Celtis yunnanensis (Yunnan Hackberry) YUNNAN PǓ
Catalpa bungei (Manchurian Catalpa)
Catalpa ovata (Chinese Catalpa)
Cercidiphyllum japonicum (Katsura Tree) LIÁN XIĀNG SHÙ
Fraxinus bungeana (Bunge Ash) XIǍO YÈ BÁI LǍ SHÙ
Fraxinus chinensis (Chinese Ash) BÁI LǍ SHÙ
Fraxinus manshurica (Manchurian Ash) SHǓI QŪ LIŪ
Ginkgo biloba (Ginkgo) YÍN XÌNG
Gleditsia sinensis (Chinese Honey Locust) ZAÒ JIÁ
Gleditsia triacanthos inermis (Thornless Honey Locust) 7 hybrids
    MĚIGÚO ZAÒ JIÁ
Larix leptolepis (Japanese Larch) RÌBEN LUÒ YÈ SÒNG
Liquidambar orientalis (Oriental Sweetgum) SŪ HÉ XIĀNG
Liquidambar styraciflua (Sweet Gum) JIĀO PÍ TANG XIĀNG SHÙ
Liquidambar taiwaniana (Taiwan Sweetgum) FĒNG XIĀNG
Liriodendron chinense (Chinese Tulip Tree) É ZHǍNG QIÚ
Metasequoia glyptostroboides (Metasequoia) SHUÌ SHĀN
Nyssa silvatica (Sourgum, Blackgum, Tupelo, Pepperidge) DUŌ HUÀ
    ZǏ SHÙ
Nyssa sinensis (Chinese Tupelo) ZǏ SHÙ

Paulownia fortunei (Fortune Paulownia) PAŌ TÓNG
Paulownia tomentosa (Royal Paulownia) BÁI MÁO TÓNG
Phellodendron amurense (Amur Cork Tree) HUÁNG BÒ
Phellodendron chinense (Smooth Chinese Cork Tree) GUĀNG YÈ
    HUÁNG PÌ SHÙ
Phellodendron japonicum (Japanese Cork Tree) RÌBEN HUÁNG BÒ
Platanus acerifolia (Maple-leaf Plane Tree) XUĀN LÍNG MÙ
Platanus occidentalis (Sycamore) MEǏGUÓ XUĀN LÍNG MÙ
Platanus orientalis (European Plane Tree) FÀGUÓ XUĀN LÍNG MÙ
Populus lasiocarpa (Chinese Poplar) DÀ YÈ YÁNG
Populus simonii (Simon Poplar) XIAǑ YÈ YÁNG
Populus szechwanensis (Sichuan Poplar) CHUAN YANG
Populus tacamahaca (Tacamac Poplar) XIĀNG CHÀNG YÁNG
Populus tremuloides (Quaking Aspen) ZHÀN YÁNG
Populus yunnanensis (Yunnan Poplar) DIĀN YÁNG
Pterocarya stenoptera (Chinese Wingnut Tree) FĒNG YÁNG
Robinia pseudoacacia (Black Locust Tree) CǏ HUAÍ
Salix babylonica (Weeping Willow) CHUÍ LIǓ
Salix matsudana tortuosa (Contorted Hankow Willow) LÓNG ZAǑ LIǓ
Sapium sebiferum (Chinese Tallow Tree) WŪ JIÙ
Sassafras albidum officinale (Sassafras) MEI ZHOU ZHA MU
Sophora japonica (Japanese Pagoda, Chinese Scholar Tree) HUAÍ SHÙ
Sophora japonica pendula (Weeping Japanese Pagoda Tree) LÓNG
    ZHAǑ HUAÍ, (DAǑ ZAǏ HUAÍ, PÁN HUAÍ)
Tilia cordata (Littleleaf Linden) XĪN YÈ DUÀN
Tilia japonica (Japanese Linden) RÌBEN DUÀN
Tilia manschurica (Manchurian Linden) KĀNG DUÀN
Ulmus parvifolia (Chinese Elm) LÁNG YÚ
Ulmus pumila (Siberian Elm) YÚ
Zelkova serrata (Japanese Zelkova) GUĀNG YÈ JǓ
Zelkova sinica (Chinese Zelkova) DÀ GUǑ JǓ

Minor Trees, Evergreen

Camellia japonica (Japanese Camellia) SHĀN CHÁ
Camellia sasanqua (Sasanqua Camellia) CHÁ SHÙ
Cassia fistula (Cassia Golden Shower Senna) Ā BÓ LÈ
Citrus aurantium amara (Bitter or Sour Orange) DAÌ DAÌ
Citrus aurantium benikoji (Benikoji Sour Orange) ZAǑ HÓNG JIÉ
Citrus aurantium limon (Rangpur Lime) NÍNG MÉNG
Citrus sarcodactylus (Buddha's Hand) FO SHO
Cleyera japonica (Japanese Cleyera) YÁNG TÓNG
Cycas revoluta (Sago Cycas) SŪ TIĔ
Ficus elastica (India Rubber Tree) YÌN DÙ XIÀNG PÍ SHÙ
Ilex vomitoria (Yaupon Holly) DAÌZHA DŌNG QĪNG
Laurus nobilis (Sweet Bay Laurel) YUÈ GUÌ
Livistona chinensis (Chinese Fan Palm) PÚ KUÍ
Magnolia grandiflora (Southern Magnolia) GUĀNG YÙ LÁN
Musa basjoo (Japanese Banana) BĀ JIĀO

Musa paradisiaca sapientum (Edible Banana) XIĀNG JIĀO, MEI REN JIĀO
Rhapis humilis (Slender Lady Palm) CĬ KUÍ
Ternstroemia gymnanthera (Japanese ternstroemia)
Trachycarpus fortunei (Fortune's Windmill Palm) ZŌNG ZHÙ

Minor Trees, Deciduous

Acer buergerianum (Trident Maple) SĀN JIĀO FĒNG
Acer ginnala (Amur Maple) CHÁ TIAO QĬ
Acer japonicum (Fullmoon Maple) RÌBEN QĬ
Acer palmatum (Japanese Maple) JI ZHUĂ QĬ
Acer palmatum atropurpureum (Redleaf Japanese Maple) HÓNG FĒNG
Acer sinense (Chinese Maple) ZHÒNG HUÁ QĬ
Cercis chinensis (Chinese Redbud) ZĬ JIĬNG
Cornus florida (Flowering Dogwood) DŌU HUÁ GOU MÙ
Cornus kousa (Japanese Dogwood) SI ZHAO HUÁ
Crataegus crus-galli (Cockspur Hawthorn) JĬ JÙ SHĀN ZHÁ
Crataegus cuneata (Nippon Hawthorn) YĚ SHĀN ZHÁ
Crataegus oxycantha (English Hawthorn) YĬNGGUÓ SHĀN ZHÁ
Crataegus phaenopyrum (Washington Hawthorn) HUÁ SHÈNG DÙN
   SHĀN ZHÁ
Diospyros kaki (Japanese Persimmon) FÉN YÈ SHÌ
Elaeagnus angustifolia (Russian Olive) ZHÁ ZĂO
Eriobotrya japonica (Loquat) PÉPA
Koelreuteria paniculata (Golden-rain Tree) LUÁN SHÙ
Lagerstroemia indica alba (White Crapemyrtle) YÍN WĒI
Lagerstroemia indica rosea (Pink Crapemyrtle) CUÌ WĒI
Litchi chinensis (Lychee) LÌ ZHĬ
Magnolia denudata (Hulan Magnolia) YÙ LÁN, YĬNG CHUN HUÁ
Magnolia liliflora (Lily Magnolia) ZĬ LÙ LÁN
Magnolia soulangeana (Saucer Magnolia) ÈR QIÁO MÙ LÁN
Magnolia stellata (Star Magnolia) RÌBEN MÚ LÁN
Malus baccata (Siberian Crab Apple) SHĀN JĬNG ZĬ
Malus halliana parkmani (Parkman Crab Apple) CHUÍ SĬ HĂI TÁNG
Malus hupehensis (Hupeh Crab Apple) HÚ BĚI HĂI TÁNG
Malus micromalus (Midget Crab Apple) XĬ FÙ HĂI TÁNG
Malus scheideckerei (Scheidecker Crab Apple) XI DE GĚ SHÍ HĂI DŌNG
Malus sieboldii (Toringo Crab Apple) SĀN YÈ HĂI DŌNG
Malus toringoides (Cutleaf Crab Apple) LÍ YÈ HĂI DŌNG
Paeonia suffruticosa (Tree Peony) MŬ DÀN or HUÁ WANG
Pistachia sinensis (Chinese Pistache) HUÁNG LIANG MÙ
Poncirus trifoliata (Hardy Orange) GOÙ JÚ
Prunus amygdalus (Almond) BĂ DÀN XÌNG
Prunus armeniaca (Apricot) XÌNG HUÁ
Prunus mume (Japanese Flowering Apricot) MEÍ HUÁ
Prunus mume alba (White Japanese Apricot) BAÍ MEÍ
Prunus persica (Peach) TAÓ
Prunus serrulata varieties (Flowering Cherries) YÍNG HUÁ
Prunus subhirtella (Higan Cherry) RÌBEN ZĂO YĬNG

Prunus triloba (Flowering Plum) MEÍ HUĀ

Prunus yedoensis (Yoshino Cherry) RÌBEN YÍNG HUĀ

Punica granatum (Pomegranate) SHÍ LIÚ

Punica granatum pleniflora (Double Red Pomegranate) CHÓNG BÁN HÓNG SHÍ LIÚ

Punica granatum multiplex (Double White Pomegranate) CHÓNG BÁN BÁI SHÍ LIÚ

Pyrus calleryana varieties (Callery Pear varieties) DOÚ LÌ

Stewartia koreana (Korean Stewartia) CHÁO XIÀN ZǏ JĪNG

Stewartia pseudocamellia (Japanese Stewartia) JIǍ SHĀN CHÁ

Styrax japonica (Japanese Snowball) YĂ MÒ LÌ

Syringa amurensis japonica (Japanese Tree Lilac) RÌBEN BÁO MÁ DING XIĀNG

Toona sinensis (Chinese Toon) XIĀNG CHŪN

Shrubs, Evergreen

Ardisia crenata (*crispa*) (Coral Ardisia) ZHŪ SHĀ GĒN

Aspidistra elatior (Cast Iron Plant) ZHĪ ZHŪ BAÒ DĀN

Aucuba japonica (Japanese Aucuba) TÁO YÈ SHĀN HÚ

Aucuba japonica variegata (Variegated Japanese Aucuba) SĂ JĪNG TÁO YÈ SHĀN HÚ

Buxus microphylla koreana (Korean Box) CHÁO XIÀN HUÁNG YÁNG

Buxus sempervirens (Common Box) JIN DÌ HUÁNG YÁNG

Cotoneaster salicifolia repens (Park Carpet Cotoneaster) JUĂN MAÓ LIǓ YÈ XUN ZÍ

Elaeagnus pungens (Thorny Elaeagnus) HÙ TŪ ZǏ

Euonymus patens (Glossy Spreading Euonymus) JIĀO ZHŌU WEÌ MÁO

Fatsia japonica (Japanese Aralia) BĀ JIǍO JĪN PÁN

Gardenia jasminoides (Cape Jasmine) ZHĪ ZÌ

Hibiscus rosa-sinensis (Chinese Hibiscus) FÚ SĀNG

Ilex crenata (Japanese Holly) PÒ YUÁN DŌNG QĪNG

Ilex crenata convexa (Convex Japanese Holly)

Ilex crenata hellerii (Heller's Japanese Holly)

Ilex cornuta (Chinese Holly) GÒU GǓ

Ilex glabra (Inkberry) GUĂN HUĀ DŎNG QĪNG

Ilex glabra compacta (Compact Inkberry)

Ilex latifolia (Lustreleaf Holly) DÀ YÈ DŌNG QĪNG

Ilex opaca (American Holly) MEÍ ZHŌU DŌNG QĪNG

Ilex pedunculosa (Longstalk Holly) CHÁNG YÈ DŌNG QĪNG

Ilex vomitoria nana (Dwarf Yaupon)

Ilex yunnanensis (Yunnan Holly) WÀN NIÁN QĪNG

Ixora chinensis (Chinese Ixora) YĪNG DĀN

Ixora coccinea (Jungle-flame Ixora) CHĒN HÓNG LÓNG CHUÁN HUĀ

Jasminum humile (Italian Jasmine) CHĀNG CHŪN XIĂO HUÁNG SU XIAN

Jasminum nudiflorum (White Jasmine) YĪNG CHŪN

Jasminum odoratissimum (Sweet Jasmine) JĪN MÓ LÌ

Jasminum officinale (Common White Jasmine) SÙ FĀNG HUĀ

Jasminum sambac (Arabian Jasmine) MÒ LÌ
Juniperus chinensis pfitzeriana (Pfitzer Juniper) LÙ JIĀO BÒ
Juniperus chinensis kaizuca (Kaizuca Juniper) LÓNG BÒ
Juniperus chinensis sargentii (Sargent's Juniper) YǍN BÒ
Juniperus communis (Common Juniper) ŌUZHŌU CǏ BÒ
Juniperus conferta (Shore Juniper) HAǏ BĪN QUÌ
Juniperus horizontalis procumbens and other creeping varieties (Creeping Junipers) PÚFÚ QUÌ
Ligustrum henryii (Henry Privet) HĒNG LÌ NǓ ZHĒN
Ligustrum japonicum (Japanese Privet) RÌBEN NǓ ZHĒN
Ligustrum lucidum (Glossy Privet) NǓ ZHĒN
Mahonia bealei (Leatherleaf Mahonia) KUÒ YÈ SHÍ DÀ GŌNG LĀO
Michelia alba (White Michelia) BAÍ LÁN HUĀ
Michelia champaca (Fragrant Michelia) HUÁNG LÁN HUĀ
Michelia fuscata (*figo*) (Banana Shrub) HÁN XIÀO
Nerium oleander (Oleander) ŌUZHŌU JIĀ ZHÚ TÁO
Osmanthus fortunei (Fortune's Osmanthus) CHǏ YÈ MÙ XĪ
Osmanthus ilicifolius (Holly Osmanthus) DŌNG SHÙ RÌBEN GUÌ HUĀ
Osmanthus serrulatus (Sweet Osmanthus) JŪ CHǏ MÙ XÍ·
Pachysandra terminalis (Japanese Spurge) DǏNG NÈI SAN JIǍO MǏ
Photinia fraserii (Fraser Photinia)
Photinia glabra (Japanese Photinia) GUĀNG YÈ SHÍ NÁN
Photinia serrulata (Chinese Photinia) SHÍ NÁN
Pieris floribunda (Mountain Andromeda) MÉIGUO MǍ JUI MÙ
Pieris japonica (Japanese Andromeda) MǍ JUI MÙ
Pinus mugo mughus (Mugo Pine) ZHÒNG OŪ SHANG SŌNG
Pittosporum tobira (Japanese Pittosporum) HAǏ TÒNG
Raphiolepis indica (Indian Hawthorn) SHÍ BĀN MÙ
Raphiolepis umbellata (Yeddo Hawthorn) SĀN YÍN SHÌ BĀN MÙ
Rhododendron catawbiense (Catawba Rhodendron)
Rhododendron hybridum (Hybrid Rhododendron) ZǍ ZHǑNG DŪ JUĀN
Rhododendron indicum (Indica Azalea) YÌNDÙ DŪ JUĀN HUĀ
Rhododendron maximum (Rosebay Rhododendron)
Rhododendron molle (Chinese Azalea) YÁNG SHǏ ZHÙ
Rhododendron mucronatum alba (Snow Azalea) MAÓ BÁI DŪ JUĀN
Rhododendron obtusum (Hiryu Azalea) SHÍ YÁN
Serissa foetida (Japanese Serissa) LIÙ YUĒ XUĚ
Skimmia japonica (Japanese Skimmia) XIĀNG YǏN YÙ
Taxus baccata repandens (Spreading English Yew)
Taxus chinensis (Chinese Yew) HOŃG DÒU SHĀN
Taxus cuspidata varieties (Japanese Yew) ZǏ SHĀN
Viburnum macrophyllum japonica (Japanese Glossy Viburnum)
Viburnum odoratissimum (Sweet Viburnum) FǍGUÓ DŌNG QĪNG
Viburnum rhitidifolium (Leatherleaf Viburnum) SHĀN PÍ PÁ

Shrubs, Deciduous

Abelia chinensis (Chinese Abelia) NUO MǏ TIÁO
Abelia grandiflora (Glossy Abelia) DÁ HUĀ LIU DAÒ MÙ

Berberis julianae (Wintergreen Barberry) LIÀNG ZHŪ CĬ

Berberis koreana (Korean Barberry) CHÁO XIĀN XIǍO NIÈ

Berberis mentorensis (Mentor Barberry) MÉN SHÌ XIAǑ NIÈ

Berberis thunbergii (Japanese Barberry) RÌBEN XIǍO NIÈ

Chaenomeles japonica (Lesser Flowering Quince) RÌBEN MÙ GUĀ

Chaenomeles lagenaria (Flowering Quince) TIĔ GĚNG HǍI TÁNG

Chimonanthus praecox (Wintersweet) LÀ MEÍ

Clethra alnifolia (Summersweet) QĪ YÈ SHĀN LĬU

Clethra barbinervis (Japanese Clethra) SHĀN LĬU

Cornus alba sibirica (Siberian Dogwood) XIBÓLÌYA RUÌ MÙ

Cornus officinalis (Japanese Cornel) SHĀN ZHŪ YÚ

Corylopsis sinensis (Chinese Corylopsis) LÀ BǍN HUĀ

Cotinus coggygria (Smoke Tree) HUÁNG LÚ

Deutzia scabra (Rough Deutzia) SOŪ SHŪ

Elaeagnus umbellata (Autumn Elaegnus) NIÚ NǍI ZĬ

Enkianthus campanulatus (Redvein Enkianthus) HÓNG MÒ DÀO ZHŌNG HUĀ

Enkianthus perulatus (Japanese Enkianthus) BAÍ DIAO ZHŌNG HUĀ

Euonymus alatus (Winged Spindle Tree) WEÌ MAÒ

Forsythia suspensa (Weeping Forsythia) LIÁN QIÁO

Forsythia viridissima (Chinese Yellow-bells) JĪN ZHŌNG HUĀ

Forsythia viridissima koreana (Korean Forsythia) CHÁO XIĀN LIÁN QIÁO

Hamamelis mollis (Chinese Witch-hazel) JĪN LǓ MEÍ

Hibiscus syriacus (Rose of Sharon) MÙ JĬN

Hydrangea macrophylla hortensia (Bigleaf Hydrangea) BĀ XIĀN HUĀ

Hydrangea quercifolia (Oakleaf Hydrangea) LI YÈ XIU QIU

Ilex verticillata (Winterberry) LUN SHENG DŌNG QĬNG

Kerria japonica (Japanese Kerria) DI TÁNG

Ligustrum obtusifolium regelianum (Regel's Privet) LĬGÉ ÉR SHÌ DUǸ YÈ SHUĬ LǍ SHÙ

Lonicera maackii (Amur Honeysuckle) JĪN YÍN MÙ

Lonicera tatarica (Tatarian Honeysuckle) TAÓ SÈ RĚN DŌNG

Nandina domestica (Nandina) NĀN TIĀN ZHÚ

Philadelphus coronarius (Sweet Mock Orange) XĪ YÁNG SHĀN MEÍ HUĀ

Philadelphus lemoinei varieties XIĀNG XUE SHĀN MEÍ HUĀ

Philadelphus purpurascens (Purple Mock Orange) ZĬ È SHĀN MEÍ HUĀ

Potentilla chinensis (Chinese Cinquefoil) WEÍ LÍNG CAÌ

Pyracantha coccinea lalandei (Laland Firethorn) OŪZHOŬ HUǑ JÍ

Rhododendron arborescens (Sweet Azalea)

Rhododendron calendulaceum (Flame Azalea)

Rhododendron nudiflorus (Pinxterbloom)

Rhododendron viscosum (Swamp Azalea)

Rhodotypos scandens (Jetbead) JĬ MǍ

Rosa banksiae (Bank's Rose) MÙ XIĀNG HUĀ

Rosa chinensis (Chinese Rose) YUÈ ZĬ

Rosa laevigata (Cherokee Rose) JĪN YĬNG ZĬ

Rosa multiflora (Japanese Rose) YÁ QIÁNG WEĪ

Rosa odorata (Tea Rose) XIĀNG SHŬI YUÈ ZÌ

Rosa roxburghii (Roxburgh Rose) CÍ LÍ
Rosa rugosa (Rugosa Rose) MEÍ GUÌ
Rosa wichuraiana (Memorial Rose) GUANG YÈ QIÀNG WĒI
Spirea cantoniensis (Reeve's Spirea) MÃ YÈ XIÙ QIÚ
Spirea japonica (Japanese Spirea) RÌBEN XIÙ XIĀN JÚ
Spirea prunifolia (Bridal Wreath Spirea) XIÃO YAN HUÃ
Syringa chinensis (Chinese Lilac) SHÍ JÍN DĪNG XIĀNG
Syringa vulgaris (Lilac) OÙZHOÙ DĪNG XIĀNG
Vaccinium corymbosum (Highbush Blueberry) SÃN FÁNG HUÃ YUÈ JÚ
Viburnum acerifolium (Mapleleaf Viburnum) QĪ YÈ JIÁ MÍ
Viburnum carlesii (Korean Spice Viburnum) KÃ LAI SHÌ JIÁ MÍ
Viburnum dilatatum (Linden Viburnum) JIÁ MÍ
Viburnum lentago (Nannyberry)
Viburnum setigerum (Tea Viburnum) TÃNG FÀNG ZÍ
Viburnum tomentosum (Doublefile Viburnum) MÚ DIÉ HUÃ
Weigela florida alba (White Old-fashioned Weigela) BAÍ JÍN DAÌ HUÃ

Vines

Akebia quinata (Five-leaf Akebia) WÚ YÈ MÙ TŌNG
Bignonia (Campsis) grandiflora (Chinese Trumpet Creeper) LÍNG XIĀO HUÃ
Bougainvillea glabra spectabilis (Bougainvillea) JIÉ HUÁNG SÃN JIAŎ HUÃ
Celastrus orbiculata (Oriental Bittersweet) NÁN SHÉ TÉNG
Clematis chinensis (Chinese Clematis) WEĪ LÍNG XIĀN
Euonymus fortunei (Wintercreeper) PÁ XÍNG WEÌ MÀO
Ficus pumila (Climbing Fig) BÍ LÌ
Hedera helix varieties (English Ivy) CHÁNG CHŪN TÉNG
Lonicera japonica chinensis (Purple Chinese Honeysuckle) HÓNG JĪN YÍN HUÃ
Lonicera japonica halliana (Hall's Honeysuckle) BAÍ JĪN YÍN HUÃ
Parthenocissus tricuspidata (Boston Ivy) PÁ SHĀN HŬ
Passiflora caerulea (Blue Crown Passion Flower) XĪ FĀN LIÁN
Trachelospermum asiaticum (Japanese Star Jasmine) RÌBEN LUÓ SHÍ
Trachelospermum jasminoides (Chinese Star Jasmine) LUÓ SHÍ
Vitis amurensis (Amur Grape) SHĀN PÚ TÁO
Vitis vinifera (European Grape) PÚ TAÓ
Wisteria sinensis (Chinese Wisteria) ZĪ TÉNG

Herbaceous and Aquatic Plants

Abelmoschus manihot (Hibiscus Manihot, Mallow) HUÁNG SHŬ KUÍ
Aconitum fischerii (Monkshood) SENG XĪE JŬ
Althaea rosea (Hollyhock) SHÙ KUÍ
Celosia cristata (Cockscomb) JI KUAN
Chrysanthemum sp. JÚ SHŬ
Commelina sp. (Day Flower) YÃ ZHÍ CAŎ SHŬ
Cymbidium ensifolium (Orchid) LÁN HUÃ
Dicentra spectablis (Bleeding Heart) YŬ RI MÙ TÁN

Epidendrum sp. (Button-hole Orchids)
Equisetum hiemale (Rat-tail) MÙ ZÉI
Fomes japonicus (Fungose Plant) LÍNG ZHÌ
Fuchsia albo-coccinea (White Fuchsia) BAǏ È DAO GUÀ JǏN ZHŌNG
Fuchsia hybrida (Hybrid Fuchsia) DIÀO ZHŌNG HUĀ
Gardenia florida (Cape Jasmine) ZHǏ ZĪ
Hemerocallis fulva (Day-lily) XUÁN HUĀ
Hosta undulata (Plantain Lily) YÙ ZĀN
Impatiens balsamina (Garden Balsam) FĒNG XIĀN HUĀ
Iris sp. CHĀNG PÚ
Iris japonica (Japanese Iris) HŪ DIÉ HUĀ
Lilium brownii (Brown's Lily) YÈ HÓ
Liriope spicata (Dwarf Lilyturf) MAÌ MÉN DŌNG
Mirabilis sp. (Four o'clock) ZÍ MÒ LÌ
Narcissus tazetta orientalis (Narcissus) SHUǏ XIĀN
Nelumbo sp. (Lotus) LIÁN HUĀ or HÓ HUĀ
Nymphaea alba (Water lily) BÁI SHUÌ LIÁN
Ophiopogon japonica (Mondo Grass) YAN JIE CAO
Orchophragmus sp. ZHU GE CAI
Paeonia sp. (Peony) SHA YAO SHU
Papaver somniferum (Opium Poppy) YING SU
Phragmites sp. (Marsh Reed) LÚ WĚI
Polygonum orientalis (Princess Feather) LIAO
Saxifraga sp. (Saxifrage) HǓ ĔR CĂO SHÙ
Thea sinensis (Tea) CHÁ YÈ HUĀ
Trapa bicornis (Water Chestnut) LÍNG HUĀ

Bamboos

Arundo donax (Giant Reed) LÚ ZHÚ
Arundo donax versicolor (White-stripe Giant Reed) HUĀ LÚ ZHÚ
Bambusa multiplex nana (Hedge Bamboo) FĒNG WEǏ ZHÚ
Chimonobambusa quadrangularis (Square Bamboo) FĀNG ZHÚ
Coix lacryma-jobi (Job's Tears) YÌ YǏ
Indocalamus latifolius KUÒ YÈ
Indocalamus or *Sassa tessalata* (Broadleaf Sassa) RUÒ ZHÚ
Phyllostachys aurea (Golden Bamboo) LUŌ HÁN ZHÚ
Phyllostachys bambusoides (Japanese Timber Bamboo) GĀNG ZHÚ
Phyllostachys bambusoides castillonis (Castillon Bamboo) HUÁNG JǏN QIÀN BÈ YÙ
Phyllostachys nigra (Black Bamboo) ZÍ ZHÚ
Phyllostachys nigra henonis (Henon Bamboo) DÀN ZHÚ
Phyllostachys pubescens (Mosa Bamboo) MAÓ ZHÚ
Phyllostachys sulphurea (Sulphur Bamboo) JǏNG ZHÚ
Pseudosassa japonica (Arrow Bamboo) SHĪ ZHÚ
Sassa senanensis (*palmata*) (Senan Bamboo) XIN NÓNG CHÌ ZHÚ
Sassa veitchi (Veitch Bamboo) WEÌ QÍ SHÌ RÙO ZHÚ
Semiarundinaria fastuosa (Narihira Cane) HǓ ZHÚ
Shibataea chinensis WŌ ZHÚ
Sinocalamus offinis (Beechey Sinocalamus) DIÀO SĪ QÍU ZHÚ

Bibliography

Chinese Gardens: Horticulture and Architecture

Attiret, Jean-Denis, *A Particular Account of the Emperor of China's Gardens Near Peking* (trans. by Sir Harry Beaumont), London, 1752.

Ayscough, Florence, 'l'Idée Chinoise d'un Jardin', *Revue des Arts Asiatique*, Paris, June 1925, pp. 39-47.

Boyd, Andrew, *Chinese Architecture and Town Planning — 1500 BC to 1911 AD*, University of Chicago Press, Chicago, 1962.

Callery, J.M., 'Architecture Chinoise; Maisons de Campagnes, Jardins', *La Revue de l'Architecture et des Travaux Publics*, vol. 17, cols, 199-207, pl. 57-9, Paris, 1859.

Chambers, Sir William, *A Dissertation on Oriental Gardening*, London, 1772.

Chen, C. 'Chinese Architectural Theory', *Architectural Review*, no. 102, pp. 19-25, July 1947.

Ch'en, H.S. and Kates, G.N., 'Prince Kung's Palace and Its Adjoining Garden in Peking', *Monumenta Serica*, 1940, vol. V, Peking.

Chi, Ch'eng, *Yuan Yeh* (*Landscape Gardening*). Treatise with Foreword dated 1634. Modern edition by The Society for Studies of Chinese Architecture, Peking, 1933.

Cibot, Frere, *Essai Sur les Jardins de Plaisance des Chinois*, Paris, 1782.

Danby, Hope, *The Garden of Perfect Brightness*, London, 1950.

Dye, Daniel Sheets, *A Grammar of Chinese Lattice*, 2 vols., Harvard-Yenching Monograph Series, vols. 5, 6, Cambridge, Mass., 1937.

Graham, Dorothy, *Chinese Gardens*, Dodd, Mead & Co., New York, 1938.

Gray, Basil, 'Buildings in Chinese Architecture', *Architectural Review*, July 1947.

Howard, Edwin, L., *Chinese Garden Architecture*, Macmillan Co., New York, 1931.

Inn, Henry and Shao, Chang-lu, *Chinese Houses and Gardens*, Bonanza Books, New York, 1940.

Jellicoe, Countess, 'Chinese Gardens', *Landscape Architectural Forum*, Winter, 1981.

Keswick, Maggie, *The Chinese Garden*, Rizzoli, New York, 1978.

Liu, Tunzhen, *Suzhou Gu Dian Yuan Lin* (*Classic Gardens of Suzhou*), Building Industry Press, Nanjing, June 1978.

Manning, Rosemary, *The Chinese Garden*, Jonathan Cape, London, 1962.

Morris, Edwin T., *The Gardens of China*, Scribner's, New York, 1983.

Murck, Alfreda and Fong, Wen, 'A Chinese Garden Court: The Astor Court at the Metropolitan Museum of Art', *MMA Bulletin*, Winter 1980-81, vol. XXXVIII, no. 3, New York, 1980.

Pane, R., 'Paesaggi e Giardini Cinesi', *Casabella*, no. 304, pp. 58-67, April 1966.

Pirazzoli-T'serstevens, Michele, *Living Architecture: Chinese*, trans. by Robert Allen, London, 1972.

Powell, Florence Lee, *In the Chinese Garden*, John Day Co., New York, 1943.

Robinson, Florence B., 'Gardens of Old China', *Country Life*, New York, April 1939.

Siren, Osvald, 'Architectural Elements of the Chinese Garden', *Architectural Review*, no. 103, pp. 251-8, June 1948.

—— *Gardens of China*, Ronald Press, New York, 1949.

—— *The Imperial Palaces of Peking*, Paris, 1926.

Thurston, Matilda, 'Beauty in Chinese Gardens', *Asia*, August 1931.

Tung, Chuin, 'Chinese Gardens in Kiangsu and Chekiang', *T'ien Hsia Monthly*, vol, 3, pp. 220-44, Nanking, 1936.

—— *Soochow Gardens*, China Building Industry Press, Nanjing, 1978.

Von Erdberg, Eleanor, *Chinese Influence on European Garden Structures*, Harvard University Press, Cambridge, Mass., 1936.

Van Henken, J.L., 'The Half-Acre Garden', *Monumenta Serica*, vol. XVIII, Peking, 1959.

Wen, Cheng-ming, *An Old Chinese Garden*, Chung Hwa Book Co., Shanghai, 1923.

Weng, Wan-go, *Gardens in Chinese Art*, China Institute, New York, 1968.

Wilson, Ernest H., *China, Mother of Gardens*, The Stratford Co., Boston, 1929.

Wrenn, Reginald, 'On Formal Gardens in China', *House & Garden*, vol. 5, pp. 139-42, 1904.

Yee, Chiang, 'Chinese Gardens', *Landscape & Garden*, vol. 2, pp. 144-8, London, 1935.

Wu, Shih-chang, 'Notes on the Origin of Chinese Private Gardens', trans. by Grace M. Boynton, *China Journal*, vol. 23, July 1935.

Chinese Art: General

Burling, Judith and Arthur Hart, *Chinese Art*, Bonanza Books, New York, and Viking Press, 1953.

Cao, Xueqin (Tsao Shwei-ch'in), *The Story of the Stone (Dream of the Red Chamber)*, vols. 1 and 2, Penguin Books, Harmondsworth, England, 1973.

Fry, Roger; Binyon, Lawrence; Siren, Osvald; Rackham, Bernard; Kendrick, A.F.; Winkworth, W.W., *Chinese Art — An Introductory Handbook to Painting, Sculpture, Ceramics, Textiles, Bronzes and Minor Arts*, B.T. Batsford Ltd, London, 1939.

Kan, Diana, *The How and Why of Chinese Painting*, Van Nostrand Reinhold Co., New York, 1974.

Liu, James J.Y., *The Art of Chinese Poetry*, University of Chicago Press, Chicago and London, 1962.

Sickman, Lawrence and Soper, Alexander, *The Art and Architecture of China*, Penguin Books, Baltimore and Harmondsworth, 1971.

Siren, Osvald, *The Chinese on the Art of Painting*, Shocken Books, New York, 1963.

Smith, Bradley and Weng, Wan-go, *China — A History in Art*, Gemini Smith Inc., and Doubleday & Co., New York, 1972.

Stein, Rolf, 'Jardins en Miniature d'Extrême-Orient', *Bulletin d'École Française d'Extrême-Orient*, 1943, pp. 1-104.

Sze, Maimai, *The Way of Chinese Painting*, Vintage Books, New York, 1959.

Watson, William, *Style in the Arts of China*, Penguin Books, Harmondsworth, England, 1974.

Willetts, William, *Chinese Art*, vol. 1, Penguin Books, Harmondsworth, England, 1958.

Williams, C.A.S., *Outlines of Chinese Symbolism and Art Motives*, Dover Publications, New York, 1976.

Chinese Religion, Philosophy, History and Biography

Alitto, Guy S., *The Last Confucian: Liang Shu-ming and the Chinese Dilemma of Modernity*, University of California Press, Berkeley, 1979.

Blofeld, John, *Taoism: The Road to Immortality*, Shambhala Publications, Boulder, Colorado, 1978.

Chan, Wing-tsit, *A Source Book in Chinese Philosophy*, Princeton University Press, Princeton, N.J., 1963.

Confucius, *The Analects of Confucius*, trans. and annotated by Arthur Waley, Vintage Books, New York, and Allen & Unwin Ltd., London, 1938.

Davis, A.R. (editor), *The Penguin Book of Chinese Verse*, Penguin Books, Harmondsworth, England, 1974.

Fung, Yu-lan, *A Short History of Chinese Philosophy*, ed. and trans. by Derek Bodde, Macmillan Co., New York and London, 1948.

Giles, H.A., *Chuang-tzu*, London, 1964.

Lin, Yutang, *My Country and My People*, Halcyon House (John Day Co.), New York, 1935.

—— *The Gay Genius — The Life and Times of Su Tungpo*, John Day Co., New York, 1947.

Malone, Carroll Browne, *History of the Peking Summer Palaces Under the Ch'ing Dynasty*, 1934.

Mather, Richard, 'Landscape and Buddhism', *Journal of Asian Studies*, vol. XVII, p. 67.

Murphey, Rhoads, 'Man and Nature in China', *Modern Asian Studies*, vol. XVIII, p. 67.

Schafer, Edward H., *The Divine Woman*, University of California Press, Berkeley, 1973 (myths about dragons, water, the female *yin*).

Shen, Fu, *Fu Sheng Liu Chi*, Taipei, 1963; trans. by Shirley Black, as *Chapters from a Floating Life*, Oxford University Press, London, 1960.

Sowerby, Arthur de C., *Nature in Chinese Art*, John Day Co., New York, 1940.

Spence, Jonathon D., *Emperor of China — Self-Portrait of K'ang-hsi*, Vintage Books (Random House), New York, 1975.

Steele, Fletcher, 'China Teaches — Ideas and Moods From Landscapes of The Celestial Empire', *Landscape Architecture*, vol. 37, pp. 88-93, April 1947.

Watson, William, *Early Civilization in China*, McGraw-Hill, New York, 1966 and Thames & Hudson, London, 1972.

Waley, Arthur, *The Life and Times of Po Chu-i*, London, 1949.

Chinese Geography

Boerschmann, Ernst, *Picturesque China*, Brentano, New York, 1923.

Nagel, *Nagel's Encyclopedia-Guide — China*, Nagel Publishers, Geneva, 1968 and later editions.

Japanese Gardens, Arts and Philosophy

Amanuma, Shinichi; Shigemori, Mirei; and Nakano, Sokei (eds.), *Teien: Kyoto Bijutsu Taikan (Gardens: Kyoto Art Survey)*, Tokyo, 1933.

Asano, Kiichi, and Takakura, Gisei, *Japanese Gardens Revisited*, Charles E. Tuttle Co., Tokyo and Rutland, VT, 1973.

Engel, David Harris, *Japanese Gardens For Today*, Charles E. Tuttle Co., Tokyo and Rutland, VT, 1959.

Engel, David Harris; Seike, Kiyoshi; Kudo, Masanobu, *A Japanese Touch For Your Garden*, Kodansha International, Tokyo 1980.

Ito, Teiji; and Iwamiya, Takeji, *The Japanese Garden: An Approach To Nature*, Yale University Press, New Haven, CT, 1972.

Hibbett, Howard, *The Floating World in Japanese Fiction*, Grove Press, New York, 1960.

Hillier, Jack, 'Japanese Drawings of the 18th and 19th Centuries', *Japan Society Newsletter*, March 1980, New York.

Drucker, Peter F., 'A Love Letter to Japanese Art', Part 1, *Japan Society Newsletter*, September 1979, New York.

Kitamura, Fumio and Ishizu, Yurio, *Garden Plants in Japan*, Kokusai Bunka Shinkokai (Society for International Cultural Relations), Tokyo, 1963.

Kitao, Harumichi, *Satei (Teahouse Gardens)*, Shokokusha, Tokyo, 1954.

Kubo, Tadashi, 'An Oldest Note of Secrets on Japanese Gardens: A Compilation of the Sakutei-ki', *Bulletin of Osaka Prefectural University*, Series B, vol. 6, 1956.

Kuck, Lorraine, *The World of the Japanese Garden: From Chinese Origins To Modern Landscape Art*, Walker/Weatherhill, New York and Tokyo, 1968, and John Day Co., 1940.

—— *One Hundred Kyoto Gardens*, Thompson (Bunkado), Kobe, 1936.

Horiguchi, Sutemi, *Katsura Rikyu (Katsura Imperial Villa)*, Mainichi, Tokyo, 1957.

Levy, Ian Hide, 'A Thousand Years of Scholarship: An Interview With Susumu Nakanishi', Japan Society Newsletter, April 1980, New York.

Hoover, Thomas, *Zen Culture*, Vintage Books (Random House), New York, 1978.

Newsom, Samuel, *A Thousand Years of Japanese Gardens*, Tokyo News Service, Tokyo, 1953.

Nishimura, Tei, *Niwa To Chashitsu (Gardens and Teahouses)*, Kodansha, Tokyo, 1957.

Okakura, Kakuzo, *The Book of Tea*, Kenkyusha, Tokyo, 1940, and Charles E. Tuttle Co., Tokyo, 1959.

Rito, Akisato, *Shinzen Teizo Den (Report on a New Selection of Gardens)*, 1828.

—— *Tsukiyama Teizo Den (Report on the Building of Artificial Hill Gardens)*, 1828.

Saito, Katsuo, *Japanese Gardening Hints*, Japan Publications, Tokyo, 1969.

—— *Niwa Tsukuri (Garden Making)* Kawade Shobo, Tokyo, 1955.

——, and Wada, Sadaji, *Magic of Trees and Stones: Secrets of Japanese Gardening*, JPT Book Co., New York and Tokyo, 1964.

Shigemori, Mirei, *Kinki Meien no Kansho (An Appreciation of Noted Gardens in the Kinki Region)*, Kyoto Inshokan, Kyoto, 1947.

Shikibu, Lady Murasaki, *The Tales of Genji* (a novel in six parts; trans. by Sumie Mishima), Kokusai Bunka Shinkokai, Tokyo, 1947.

Tamura, Tsuyoshi, *Art of the Landscape Garden in Japan* (trans. by Sumie Mishima), Kokusai Bunka Shinkokai, Tokyo, 1947.

—— *Jardin Japonais:Ses Origines et Caracteres, Dessins et Plans*, Kokusai Bunka Shinkokai, Tokyo, 1939.

Yoshinaga, Yoshinobu, *Nihon no Teien (Japanese Traditional Gardens)*, Shokokusha, Tokyo, 1958.

Watts, Alan, W., *The Way of Zen*, Pantheon, New York, 1957.

Yoshimura, Yuji, and Halford, Govanna M., *The Japanese Art of Miniature Trees and Landscapes: Their Creation, Care and Enjoyment*, Charles E. Tuttle Co., Tokyo and Rutland, VT, 1957.

Index